ECO
HARMONY DAWN
COOKING

BALANCING YOUR INTERNAL
& EXTERNAL ENVIRONMENTS

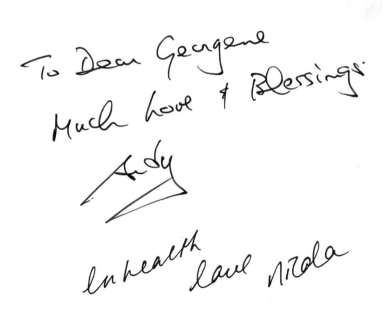

To Dear Georgene
Much Love & Blessings

Judy

In health
Dave Nicola

ECO HARMONY DAWN COOKING

BALANCING YOUR INTERNAL & EXTERNAL ENVIRONMENTS

NICOLA LAWRENCE
ANDY JAMES

Published by:
First Choice Books
#2, 460 Tennyson Place
Victoria, BC
V8Z 6S8
www.firstchoicebooks.ca

National Library of Congress Cataloging
Lawrence, Nicola and James, Andy
Eco Harmony Dawn Cooking: Balancing your Internal and External Environments
ISBN 9781926747447

Inquiries to the authors may be directed to Harmony Dawn Retreat Centre, www.harmonydawn.com.

The highest form of goodness is like water.
Water knows how to benefit all things without striving with them.
It stays in places loathed by all men.
Therefore, it comes near the Tao.

In choosing your dwelling, know how to keep to the ground.
In cultivating your mind, know how to dive in the hidden deeps.
In dealing with others, know how to be gentle and kind.
In speaking, know how to keep your words.
In governing, know how to maintain order.
In transacting business, know how to be efficient.
In making a move, know how to choose the right moment.

If you do not strive with others,
You will be free from blame.

Tao Te Ching

For my parents Derek and Margaret for their beautiful souls, their tireless help on all fronts, and for their belief in us and Harmony Dawn.

To the memory of Andy's mom Beryl, granny or Auntie Noo Noo for her superb culinary genius to which I am forever indebted and for her incredible disposition, which we all miss tremendously.

~Nicola

ACKNOWLEDGEMENTS

First and foremost, our deepest, heartfelt thanks go to our dear friend and web genius, Lin Taylor of LT Designs, for her incredible work designing our book. Ever creative, she goes out of her way to truly reflect who we are and what our work is about…. and effectively get it out to the wide World! Who can ask for more?

Harmony Dawn's acclaimed cuisine could not be sustained at such a high level without consistent support in the kitchen. We would like to thank Angela Allen and Corinne Patterson (of Lionheart Bread Making Studio) for their excellent culinary skills, hard work, genuine friendship and good times in helping us turn out the many Harmony Dawn faves. To my sous chef parents who are always in demand from guests when they assist, a heart felt thank you!

Thanks to Dr. Melissa West for her Foreword, continuing support and friendship, Jennifer Corris for her marketing and advertising help, Susie Dias of East to West Yoga and Joanne Lowe of The Big Stretch Yoga.

Thanks to our family and friends for their support, love and friendship and for being my testers.

To the hundreds of guests who have come through our doors since we opened in 2003, we are immensely grateful for the positive feedback, support, smiles and kindness.

FOREWORD

Harmony Dawn retreat centre is a symbiotic space that allows us to become open and mindful of our human interaction with our environment. At a time when environmentalism has become a trendy marketing technique, Harmony Dawn is truly a place of sustainable healthy living that allows us to connect our internal and external environments in a harmonious and life-affirming way. Nicola and Andy are gracious hosts who have created a welcoming space that invites us to reflect on our deeper inner life and thus allow us to move outward into the world in a more conscious and responsible way.

One of the highlights of anybody's stay at Harmony Dawn is the tasty, wholesome, and gratifying food. Harmony Dawn is a place of balance and equilibrium where the philosophy of harmony extends to every aspect of living including the dinner plate. Nicola Lawrence lovingly prepares meals in a way that both nurtures and nourishes our bodies, minds and souls. With her delicious cooking and recipes Nicola demonstrates that the choices we make about food are powerful tools not only for inner transformation but also for sustainable living. Harmony Dawn cooking allows us to connect our inner values of loving kindness and compassion to our actions and offers an example of how to live with honesty and integrity as global citizens.

Harmony Dawn has deeply influenced my own way of thinking and acting as part of the world. From food and environmental choices to my yoga practice and teachings, Harmony Dawn has taught me first hand, there is no out there and in here... we are all one.

Dr. Melissa West Yoga Teacher and Host of Returning to the Body Mind on Contact Talk Radio

MORE PRAISE FOR HARMONY DAWN

We would like to extend our deepest gratitude to both of you for our inspiring weekend at Harmony Dawn. Nicola, you filled our bellies with nature's bounty which you transformed into a sumptuous adventure for our palates. As our bellies were nourished so too were our souls, as we breathed in the ambiance of reverence and pure potentiality at Harmony Dawn. Our international travels have taken us to many great places, Harmony Dawn now ranks among our very favorite.
Namaste,
~ Shelley and Gail – The Compassionate Sisters

I truly had no idea how impactful this weekend would be on my life. I did not see that coming. I thought I was coming to hang out. What you have created with Andy is truly magical. I am already broadcasting, this was a dynamic weekend. The work, the love, the commitment, this is a very powerful, profound, life-changing, altering experience. I am overwhelmed by your actions, the way you are living your life by example, and truly vehemently supportive. It fits in with where I want to go for sure. The food, the menus, the friendships - that teamwork again, what a phenomenal experience. I loved every minute moment to moment.
~ Patty Parsons – HD Cooking Workshop Participant

This past weekend was a very special and memorable experience at Harmony Dawn for me. I cannot begin to thank you both for the warmth, compassion, care and thoughtfulness that you put into making this retreat something that shall stay with me forever. I had no idea of what I was getting myself into when I showed up on the Friday evening, but I immediately was put at ease and felt very comfortable in the silence and reflective nature of the weekend. Last, but certainly not least, I would like to thank you Nicola for the wonderful meals that you provided us with. I have never tasted food so wonderful - as I have mentioned, I have been to some of the best restaurants and spas in the world (Canyon Ranch in Arizona, St. Annes in Cobourg, Banff Springs in Alberta, Grail Springs in Grafton, James

Beard House in New York, etc.) but by far, you have surpassed anything I have ever tasted. It felt like my mouth was throwing a party for my face with each bite I took! I have already talked to 4 of my friends.
~ Tracy Wallace – Particpant in Andy's Meditation & Qigong Retreat

I wanted to express my gratitude to you and Andy for the extraordinary commitment you both have brought to making Harmony Dawn the exceptional retreat experience that it was for me. The competence, impeccability, creativity and compassion with which you and Andy fulfilled your roles as hostess and teacher created a space in which I was able to rediscover and renew my commitment to my practice and to return to the challenges of my life empowered and refreshed. So, thank you both. You guys give great Space. Cheers.
~ Michael Bauhaus – Bauhaus Windows

We were truly impressed by Harmony Dawn centre. While majority talk about protection of the environment, you two put it together on ground in a beautiful way. Andy's quiet energy and your dynamic active force are complementary and it reminds me of Yin Yang balance.
~ Pradeep Kumar – Meditation Teacher

"Nicola's food is truly inspiring. Every time I host a retreat at her centre, I highlight the innovative menu as one of the greatest attractions. Consistently, my participants leave giving rave reviews and inspired to embrace a more vegetarian based diet. Her meals are simple, yet stunning. The flavours combine in a way that takes your breath away. It is so rare that you find someone who has fused passion and flavour so well with health...and don't even get me started on the desserts... divine! Her cookbook is ideal for anyone who wants to embrace a new and healthier style of cooking."
~ Colin Matthews Director – Kula Yoga Oakville

The wonderful , profound energy of Harmony Dawn has left a lasting impression on my body, mind and spirit. I haven't encountered this type of profound shift in my healing journey until now. Your spirit, the nurturing meals, combined with Andy's qigong massage has had an interesting effect on my body and emotional state since returning. I am still getting used to a new self. I sincerely hope I can come back soon, Many thanks for sharing this wonderful space. Blessings,
~ Connie – Yoga Student

I just wanted to take a moment to thank you both for a beautiful week-end! It was absolutely breath taking, inspiring, loved everything, the yoga, meditation, great conversations and what can I say the FOOD was divine! I am thrilled with my new cook book! Nicola, your parents were delightful, I thoroughly enjoyed meeting both of them!
~ Mar – HD Cleansing Qigong Retreat Particpant

Thank you for a most enjoyable weekend! Lovely people, incredible food, beautiful surroundings and an opportunity to learn something new, how could it not be wonderful.
~ Elva – HD Cooking Workshop Participant

TABLE OF CONTENTS

TABLE OF CONTENTS

TABLE OF CONTENTS

TABLE OF CONTENTS

Welcome to Harmony Dawn

My first book *The Dao of Harmony Dawn Cooking: Innovative and Acclaimed Spa Cuisine* came out in the spring of 2007. It was a labour of love for all the wonderful people I have had the pleasure to meet and feed since our doors opened in 2003. At that time, I had no idea that within a short year and a half, I would find myself writing my second book. However with my recipe list always growing and more "Please can I have the recipe?" requests, I felt that perhaps the time was right to think of a new project. My initial feeling was I didn't want the book to be solely about the food I prepare for our guests, because Harmony Dawn is not just about food, it is about the experience you feel when you are here.

Eco Harmony Dawn Cooking: Balancing your Internal and External Environments was born out of the collaboration between Andy and myself, both coming from different angles, but both sharing the same collective goal of wanting to do something better for us and the planet. The retreat itself is an experiential example of what we are trying to convey and accomplish and it is my hope that this book will transcend the page and take you into our world at Harmony Dawn, which is spirit of food, spirit of community and spirit of balance.

Nicola Lawrence & Andy James

ECOLOGY: EXTERNAL & INTERNAL

INTRODUCTION

Food is a big part of the Harmony Dawn experience as evidenced by our many testimonials and the brisk and continued sales of Nicola's *The Dao of Harmony Dawn Cooking: Innovative and Acclaimed Spa Cuisine*. However, guests repeatedly ask about the thinking that went into creating Harmony Dawn and how they too can take steps to eat and live more healthily and sustainably. They intuitively sense that sustainable living is part of healthy living, individually and collectively.

So here it is - ***Eco Harmony Dawn Cooking***! "Eco" in this context is short for "Ecology" and more particularly, Human Ecology. Human Ecology, which is defined by the Concise Oxford Dictionary as "the study of the interaction of people with their environment", is a relatively young science, becoming a separate field of study only in the 1970s. In other words, it was only about 30 years ago that our leading thinkers finally figured out that human beings were impacting their environment - both natural and artificial – and in turn being impacted. Ecology is still not a common field of study, even as the evidence of serious global environmental crises mount – global warming triggering rapid climate changes, water, food and energy shortages, environmental degradation, pollution of air, water and land, and more. Add to this, the rapid widening of the volatile, poverty gap, the runaway implementation of science and technology, and of course the ever-present threat of one country or even a small group (enabled by technology) inflicting massive damage.

The interactive Eco theme seems particularly apt for this book, since it is an important element not only in our cuisine, but in the creation and on-going operation of Harmony Dawn itself. Conventionally, ecology books and studies treat the "environment" as external to the individual. At Harmony Dawn, we certainly acknowledge the vital importance of human interaction with our external environments – both natural and artificial - and the need for urgent changes therein. In addition and perhaps unconventionally, we also point out that individuals interact with and indeed, are propelled by their "internal" environment - body, emotions, energy, mind, and spirit.

Moreover, it seems clear to us that the internal and external environments are themselves interconnected in many ways, which we will explore in this book.

Life is becoming increasingly complex, which for most people also means more stressful and confusing. However, as the 20th century sage J.D. Krishnamurti pointed out, we cannot overcome complexity with even more complexity – more specialization, bureaucracy etc. - but only with simplicity. If we understand our deeper, inner dynamics (our inner ecology), we will come to fundamental human issues and in that sense, our choices will become simpler.

Food is a prime example of the interaction of inner and outer. It is something "external" we ingest into our bodies, which then affects our internal chemistry, energetics, moods, health etc. These internal factors subsequently influence our interactions with the external world, including how we produce food… and so the circles go.

At Harmony Dawn, most of our guests instinctively or intuitively grasp these interconnections as a reality. Our Meditators, Yogis, Tai Chi practitioners, mystics and others are obviously focused on their personal, "internal" exploration and transformation, but are also clearly concerned about the quality of the environments we humans have created in the name of progress and prosperity. This sensitivity to both internal and external realities, keep drawing them to the nurturing environment of Harmony Dawn.

In this book and in our on-going work at Harmony Dawn, we explore and work with the particulars of life's many interconnections. The more clearly we see these interconnections, the more obvious it becomes that indeed "We are One", not only idealistically, but practically and specifically. We are One with Others, with our Environment and especially with our Food, whether we think of this as nourishment, pleasure, socializing or community building.

WE ARE ONE

It is a shame that the saying, "We are One" (or variations thereof like the superstar global hit, "We are the World") has been so over-used and at times abused, it has now become trite and meaningless to many. "We are One" happens to be a reality on several different levels and it is a truth we need to urgently apply in our increasingly complex, interrelated and challenging world. If the world is really to be transformed, the feeling and clear understanding that, "We are One" must be sustained beyond one single issue, one single leader (no matter how shining) or one single crisis. It must be both a guiding vision and an ongoing realization, relevant to all issues at all times.

Although a growing number of people proclaim themselves as "global" or "world" citizens, polls show that the overall numbers are still relatively small and in addition, people's actions have consistently fallen short of their stated global values. In other words, many so-called global citizens are not there as yet. Just within the last decade or so, for example, there has been widespread media coverage, excitement and popular support in North America (and far beyond) for the 1997 Kyoto Protocol and subsequently for Al Gore's 2006 "Inconvenient Truth" climate change project. The enthusiasm for both of these promising global initiatives evaporated relatively quickly under George W. Bush, giving way to worries about the "economy" and additionally, the fear-mongering, on-going, and ever-shifting "war on terrorism"....whatever that was or is.

In this context, two facts should be noted. Firstly, the ecological/ environmental movement in Europe (and certain other parts of the planet) is much stronger and more consistent than in North America, boasting many practical successes, which have garnered relatively little media coverage in North America, especially the USA. The Green Movement is not necessarily a muddled-headed dive into economic disaster as many North American pundits predict. Secondly, although George W. Bush was an environmentalist's worst nightmare, we in the West have found a wide range of excuses over the last 30 years for our inaction concerning the gathering global storms. In other words, we the ordinary people, have to step up and take responsibility for our decisions and for our planet, not only through voting, but spending and more.

The urgent question for Humanity is not so much if we need a much higher level of compassion and cooperation, but how can we get to that level? Over his twenty-five years of teaching and even before that, Andy has pointed out that while it is a great impetus to have inspiring global leaders with integrity, compassion and vision - like Mahatma Gandhi, the Dalai Lama, Mother Theresa, Nelson Mandela and now perhaps, Barack Obama – it is also necessary for the average person to radically change. Each of us needs to transform her or his consciousness in order to recognize appropriate leadership and support it on an on-going basis, through seeming highs and lows. Without this continuing support, the end result of any Great Leader's work will be more of the same - one step forward and one step back; one step to the left and one step to the right. Meanwhile, our global, human crises will continue to escalate.

There are many specific reasons for the gap between our ideals and actions, but perhaps the deepest and most universal is that we feel ourselves to be separate from each other, from our natural environment, and from our Divine Oneness… or "God" to many. We struggle to bridge the gap. Such feelings of alienation have not been as prominent in all cultures and eras as they are in ours, wherein our current embrace of Science and Capitalism accentuates separation, fragmentation and competition, rather than integration and cooperation. In short, modern society tends to exaggerate the processes which break us into competitive parts, rather than uniting us into a Whole. These processes operate on us both individually and collectively.

We are at an unique point in human history, wherein our practical, global challenges as well as our most profound, spiritual teachings, are calling us to the same place – to unite on a common, higher human ground.

To be able to step unto that higher ground, we must expand the dimensions and parameters of what it means to be "I" and our particular collective identity as, "We" whether that is defined by political ideology, nationality, race or religion. This expansion of the sense of self is essentially a matter of spiritual transformation and shifting of consciousness and will not come about merely through more information or substituting one belief for

WE ARE ONE

another. At this point, we run into an ironic and very substantial obstacle.

Popular religions, which we would expect to be calling for more humanity and compassion, have over the past few decades, been responsible for increasing religious intolerance and conflict. Although, the extremists are probably a small minority, they have not been restrained by the majority and are succeeding in their destructive work of polarization.

Perhaps the problem is one of belief or "faith". There is a strong current of teaching in the Abrahamic (acknowledging the same lineage of prophets going back to Abraham) religions - Judaism, Christianity and Islam - which asserts that the way to salvation is through fervent belief, even unto martyrdom. It seems that a significant majority of believers treat their respective holy books as accurate historical records and as literally the Word of God. The moderates may try to moderate the content of their extremist brothers' and sisters' belief systems, but rarely question the dynamic and process of Belief itself. They therefore cannot initiate substantial change within their own religions nor resolve conflict with other organized religions.

Belief is not transformational. Indeed, it tends to promote rigidity, since questioning religious belief is often taken as questioning the religion itself or perhaps even challenging the "Word of God". It also entrenches conflict, since Believers immediately create their own shadows, dark side, antagonists - the Non-believers. The interactions between George W. Bush and Osama bin-Laden immediately after the 9/11 attacks were a classic example of this process of mutual demonization. This is not an encouraging dynamic, since Christians and Muslims together account for more than half the world's population.

At the end of his 2003 book, *Ageless Wisdom Spirituality: Investing in Human Evolution,* Andy called for a more profound and open-minded public discussion of the role of spirituality and religion, which would include the examination of matters like belief. Even now, the atmosphere is still so charged, representatives of the organized religions generally shy away from controversial issues. Regularly on TV, pundits only have to quote from their respective holy books to put an end to inquiry and questioning.

Their pronouncements are rarely challenged unless they are advocating outright violence or war. This trepidation is understandable, but without going deeper, unresolved conflicts will continue to be scattered across our collective landscape, creating a minefield for the future. If we cannot talk to each other in times of relative peace and prosperity, what will happen when conditions deteriorate?

Andy's call for a more evolved exploration of spirituality within society was answered even before *Ageless Wisdom Spirituality* (AWS) was formally launched. A long time friend, Eli Bay, synchronistically called (without knowing about AWS) to encourage Andy to join the Forge Guild, an international group of spiritual teachers and leaders who advocated "trans-traditional" spirituality. It seemed uncanny.

Not long after joining the Forge, Andy was invited by its founder, Dr. Robert Forman to join a Think Tank or Design Team of Forge Guild members, who would meet bi-coastally in the USA to inquire into if and how a more evolved spirituality could positively impact politics and society. This was early 2005, and Bush was just coming back for a second term of hard-ball, divisive, partisan politics. The Religious Right was a powerful force then (and still is) and of course Islamic extremists around the world were bent on creating havoc. In many quarters, people shied away from the very words, "religion" and "spirituality".

The Design Team, initially eighteen in number, was a most impressive, talented and diverse group – spiritual teachers and leaders, psychologists, educators, corporate facilitators, authors and more. This process of inquiry, brain-storming and discussion eventually took 18 months, including face to face meetings, emails and phone calls. The agenda was absolutely open and the exchanges were profound, passionate and at times, discordant, since there were political and personality differences as well as specialization preferences.

The eventual outcome of this creative process was the **"Call to Global Spiritual Citizenship",** quoted hereinafter in its entirety:

We Are One

"Our urgent worldwide challenges cry out for nothing less than a guiding vision that transcends political polarities and sectarian divisions. Humanity is being called to a new way of being that reflects the reality of our essential oneness. Embracing such a transformation of consciousness can inspire genuine cooperation and generate solutions that satisfy both our deep spiritual longings and our practical needs. The core of the world's wisdom traditions – and the leading edge of modern science – point to the following principles as the basis for such an approach:

- **All beings are endowed with the infinite energy** that is the source of life itself, and which we call by different names, both religious and secular.
- **Forging a conscious connection** to this ultimate reality is an innate part of the human drive for meaning, wholeness, and fulfillment.
- **Deepening that connection** can enhance our innate capacity for wisdom, kindness, love, and other universal virtues.
- **No single tradition**, philosophy or faith is the only way to describe or satisfy this basic drive for profound meaning and higher purpose.

Imagine a world in which these principles guide not only our personal lives but social and political as well.

We of the Forge Institute – spiritual leaders, teachers and practitioners from a wide range of paths – believe that such a world is possible if we reach across the boundaries of belief, ethnicity and nationality to tap the sacred source that unites all. Standing on that firm foundation, we can address our collective problems by harvesting the best resources of all systems of knowledge - spiritual, technological and scientific – while recognizing that no one perspective contains all the truth for all cultures, times and conditions. We invite people from all corners of the world to affirm the above principles and pledge to realize the following moral imperatives:

- **Acknowledge and treat as sacred** the interconnectedness of all living beings to each other and to our beloved planet.
- **Build relationships**, families, and communities that foster complete human development in every domain of life.
- **Enlarge our circle of concern**, expanding what we think of as "I" and "we" to embrace the well-being of others as part of our own well-being.
- **Stand firm in favor of religious and spiritual freedom** – and against religion-based coercion or violence.
- **Form governments that rise above partisan ideologies** to creatively address our needs for security, prosperity and justice while also protecting freedom, health and the environment.
- **Develop our capacity**, individually and together, to bring these ommitments into reality.

We humbly urge you to join us in a sincere and determined effort to develop initiatives, both public and private, that boldly address our common challenges."

Andy is very passionate about *"The Call"* not only because it is very much in alignment with his earlier works and writings, but also because this document was the result of a genuine, conscious, creative, interactive, drag-it-out process between many accomplished, spiritual human beings. No one in this design team knew what the eventual outcome would be. Many different kinds of initiatives, big and small, were discussed. *"The Call"* is the eventual Fruit.

At the most basic level, **The Call to Global Spiritual Citizenship (GSC),** (www.globalspiritualcitizenship.org) is a petition for more evolved spirituality within society and politics, which can subsequently be taken to leaders in all spheres of life, including President Obama. The Forge is working on specific applications of the GSC and welcomes cooperation with other groups which are similarly engaged. The GSC also points to how the Individual's (the "I") spiritual transformation may evolve and how that process might in turn impact the specifics of our Collective life

WE ARE ONE

(the "We") – politics, economics, health, environment and more. If the GSC resonates with you, please sign up, share it with your friends and colleagues and if appropriate, align your organization with the GSC.

INTERNAL ECOLOGY: THE SOURCE

In the preceding section, "We are One", it was proposed that a shift of consciousness within individuals is necessary for us to rise to our urgent global challenges. This same shift is necessary even if you are primarily focused on raising the quality of your individual life and your family's – finding meaning, building loving and nurturing relationships, and enjoying robust mind-body health. Indeed, the collective shift cannot occur without a shift within many individuals.

All our actions, whether we choose to categorize them as private, public, scientific, technological, economic, leisure, religious, political, charitable, cultural etc., come from inside ourselves and all of them impact our various 'external' environments, which in turn influence our thoughts and actions. Yet few of us have really inquired into the Source or Centre from which all our thoughts, words and actions tumble out, often in haphazard fashion. Great spiritual teachers and philosophers over the millennia have pointed to this common lack of self-knowledge and its profound implications. Socrates was unequivocal: "The unexamined life is not worth living".

Many people argue that all our imperfections, including our lack of self-knowledge, are simply part of 'human nature' and that humanity has survived innumerable crises over the ages. Although this is true, hereunder are a few points to consider in response to this line of thinking.

Firstly, the fact that humanity has survived in the past does not guarantee survival now. The speed and scale of scientific and technological innovation have pushed us and our planet to unprecedented limits. Global population has exploded and now tops 6 billion; the oceans and the atmosphere are heavily polluted and are reaching tipping points; land, food, energy and fresh water are in limited supply; the planet is rapidly warming, a process which is already triggering volatile and extreme climate change. The technology and weaponry of the 21st century will develop at an exponential rate and with it, the possibility of catastrophic wars, terrorist attacks or accidents of unprecedented scale.

Secondly, most human beings do not live their lives in terms of centuries

INTERNAL ECOLOGY: THE SOURCE

or millennia, but in much shorter increments of years, months, weeks or even days. Excusing the foibles of human nature over the millennia does not help us solve any problems now, on either the individual or collective level. The actual and immediate challenge every moment always is, "We have to act now. What do we do?" To say, "Let's do what we have always done, because at least it's familiar" is a neither rational nor appropriate response.

Thirdly, what we call 'human nature' can and does change, and it is possible (although not easy) to direct that change. Human nature is extremely complex and is rarely, if ever, investigated at a profound level within the popular media. Most of us have little time to look into ourselves because we are busy trying to find happiness and fulfillment outside of ourselves…which of course is impossible in the long term.

Change can be either 'horizontal' or 'vertical'. Most of the kinds of change with which we are familiar are horizontal. We constantly swap politicians, fashions, ideologies, beliefs, jobs and even spouses and partners; the economy goes up and down; international tensions rise and fall; there is a constant influx of new information, new celebrities and technological toys to excite us; we gain or lose weight; we get older. If it seems, however, that our fundamental human dynamics ('nature') never really change, that seemingly cynical perception is largely true, which is why this kind of change is described as 'horizontal'. We strive mightily, but stay on the same level of consciousness and behaviour, and so keep reliving similar kinds of problems, albeit with different specifics.

'Vertical' or 'transformational' change among mature adults is much needed, but relatively rare, especially since few people seem to be even aware of the concept or possibility. One of the purposes of the GSC and of Andy's present work, is to point to this possibility, not only because it is desperately needed in the world now, but because it has been the underlying message of the world's great spiritual teachers – to become conscious of the divine within ourselves, which is our deepest identity. However, as Gautama Buddha taught, even Buddhas can only point the way. In other words, the realization of a more enlightened consciousness ultimately depends on our own efforts.

Vertical change may be viewed as an expansion of the sense of self or 'I'. Ken Wilber points to the various levels of human development from birth to childhood, adolescence and on to adulthood as an example of this process. At each new level, the sense of self expands and new faculties are activated. But why should the expansion of consciousness come to a dead halt once we reach adulthood? The leading edges of Psychology are now straying into traditional 'spiritual' territory by beginning to acknowledge that consciousness can indeed keep evolving, expanding the sense of self and "I" beyond the conventional.

Many of our present collective challenges, both national and international, can be met if we evolve to just the next level of consciousness whereby we truly think and act as global citizens. But this expansion/ transformational shift needs conscious inner - oriented work, which has traditionally been regarded as "spiritual", hence the name of the GSC initiative – Global Spiritual Citizenship. It should be pointed out that consciousness can expand way beyond this global level, but that discussion deserves a separate book.

There are two main spiritual, transformational paths – The Heart (devotion) and the Head (wisdom). The overwhelming majority of human beings are drawn to the heart-devotional path because emotion is powerful, ever-present in our lives, and it often overrides our reason. A personalized relationship with the Divine/ God may make us feel special, sacred, elevated, cared for and reassured, especially in hard times, and this would undoubtedly give us hope and sustenance, which of course is positive. All three Abrahamic religions, Judaism, Christianity, and Islam, are devotional, as well as most of Hinduism.

However, as we discussed in the "We are One" section, devotional religion which remains rigidly belief-based and focused on an exclusive, external god is rarely transformational and has repeatedly given rise to conflict and even war, as one religion's belief and god are set against another's. Often, underlying our polite, religious protestations of peace are dynamics of division.

INTERNAL ECOLOGY: THE SOURCE

It does not seem to be widely known that mystics and higher level practitioners of devotional paths, east and west, recognize and realize that the Divine is not only outside of themselves (transcendent) but within as well (immanent), which points to the reality, "We are One". This concept of the divine is familiar in the East, especially within Hinduism, but is much rarer in the West, where many prominent mystics over the ages have been killed for the "blasphemy" of claiming that the divine spark could exist in mere mortal creatures. Even today within certain sections of Islam, the mystic Sufi sects are shunned.

The Wisdom path, which includes Hinduism's Jnana Yoga and much of Buddhism, is more direct and much less travelled. This approach brings penetrating, objective awareness and attention to whatever is rising and falling, moment by moment, within our consciousness, including our 'I' thoughts. The process of seeing ever deeper and more clearly into 'what is' - both inside and outside of ourselves - and letting go of whatever is illusory or false, has been likened to peeling the layers of an onion or stripping away the wrapping around a light bulb. In this way, we can come to the Source even without having as a conscious goal, personal enlightenment or union with god. As our self-erected barriers dissolve, we increasingly feel and see our subtle interconnections with others and with our environment generally.

Both the Heart and Head paths, if sincerely and consistently followed, lead to the same place and indeed have been described by some teachers not as separate paths but different aspects of the same path. They both involve letting go of attachment to and identification with the sense of the individual 'I' or ego, with its beliefs, attitudes, attachments and identifications. This does not mean we should try to eradicate the conventional 'I' or ego and go live in a cave. We need an ego in order to function within society. However, the conventional ego is not all that the 'I' or self is. It is capable of expanding to the level of a global citizen and beyond. In so doing, we begin to see life in 'both-and' terms rather than linear 'either-or'; we begin to see different levels of reality operating at the same time. As our sense of 'I' expands, so too do our hearts and feelings of compassion. Andy's original and main meditation teacher, Dhiravamsa, describes this more evolved sense of 'I' as the 'aware ego'.

Power in the sense of our "ability to do or act" has two main components. The most familiar, pursued and used are what might be described as 'tools and resources', whether these are seemingly 'external' like brute strength or size, wealth, education, charisma, and beauty or 'internal' like will, focus, intelligence, drive, ruthlessness, natural talent etc.

The second component of power, which does not seem to be widely recognized, is 'wisdom'. This is the ability to use our tools and resources in a balanced way and to adapt them to constantly changing circumstances. Our tools and resources are neutral and can be used positively or negatively, as we can see in both individuals and groups.

These tools or abilities do not guarantee happiness or harmony, although they are commonly rewarded by society because they 'get things done'. Transformational self-knowledge investigates the user of those tools, (the 'I'), which in its conventional, unexamined state tends towards rigidity, resistance to change and identification with various beliefs, fads and personae. To charge into activity without knowing who we truly are, is to put the proverbial cart before the horse. This dynamic is the norm today at all levels of society.

The Buddha seemed to be pointing to these same components of power when he distinguished between two basic streams of Meditation, which may be seen as forms of inner power or potential: 1) Concentration, focus or one-pointedness (Samatha). 2) Wisdom (Vipassana).

One-pointedness is powerful, as we can see in a laser beam, a fire hose or indeed in people who are 'single-minded'. In meditation, it leads to trance states and sometimes extraordinary powers. However, it does not necessarily lead to wisdom and light. It is possible to be one-pointed, possessed of extraordinary abilities and yet evil – like the evil sorcerer, black magician or fallen angel.

INTERNAL ECOLOGY: THE SOURCE

Vipassana means to 'see' with the utmost, direct clarity - in, through and around - so that action flows spontaneously. We 'see' by paying attention with keen awareness to whatever is taking place within consciousness, moment by moment. This awareness includes both 'external' and 'internal' phenomena including the operation of our 'I'. Unlike Samatha practice, nothing is excluded from consciousness; there is an attitude of hospitality and acceptance. No explanation is imposed on what is seen; there is no 'doing'. Out of this no-doing, out of space and emptiness, arises deep, penetrating insight, which guides us in using our tools, abilities, knowledge and resources.

In this section, we have focused mostly on the transformation of the 'I' or ego, which directs all our actions. Some spiritual and religious traditions focus on this process exclusively through prayer, meditation, ritual etc., even to the extent of neglecting the body.

Other spiritual traditions, which may broadly be called 'tantric', embrace the whole human being. For example, Indian Raja Yoga and modern Chinese Qigong contain comprehensive techniques which focus on the body and physical postures, vital energy (prana or qi), and various forms of meditation, which we have been discussing above. In other words, they embrace the integration of body, energy, mind and beyond. The physical and energetic techniques may be likened to tools, abilities and resources. The various meditation techniques (hopefully) enable us to investigate the mind and the 'I'. In a sense, the 'I' is 'higher' and in control. However, at the same time, body, energy and mind are all interconnected, with each part affecting every other part. Thus the function of the 'I' is not always to control but sometimes to let go... like a wise parent, who recognizes that she or he knows a lot, but is not all-knowing or omnipotent. Sometimes the parent can learn from the child.

EXTERNAL ECOLOGY AND FOOD

What practical steps could we, with a truly, more evolved global consciousness, take to build more sustainable, compassionate and healthier societies? Many changes would automatically flow from such a shift in consciousness, since we would accept as 'hard-headed reality', the fact that the universe is much more subtly interconnected than we presently acknowledge. We would see with different eyes and would therefore choose and act accordingly.

Our current measure of 'reality' is not 'obvious' as many assume, but is the legacy of 400 years of modern science, which is relatively fleeting in terms of human history. The scientific method breaks life down into ever smaller conceptual boxes and seeks to establish measurable and direct, cause-and-effect relationships within them. This undoubtedly works extremely well in controlled laboratory experiments and has led to rapid scientific and technological innovation, which has dramatically transformed our planet and our lives.

However, it does not work so well for our general quality of life when we unthinkingly and automatically apply it in our courts, government offices, schools, universities and corporate board rooms. In real life outside the lab, everything is much more complex. Issues are not stringently controlled and isolated, but interconnected and constantly changing. Think about George W. Bush's attempt to convert Iraq to compliant, western democracy through military force, while demonizing Islam, destroying Iraq's infrastructure and killing many tens or even hundreds of thousands of innocent Iraqis, casually dismissed as 'collateral damage'! If you were an Iraqi (think American or Canadian in similar circumstances), would you be compliant?

There may be and usually are, multiple (not single), constantly interacting causes and effects. Such relationships may be difficult or expensive (usually unaffordable to individuals) to measure; they may contain a 'subjective' element – personal feelings and perceptions, about which we are currently ambivalent and relatively ignorant, since we focus most of our research and investigation on the 'external' world.

EXTERNAL ECOLOGY AND FOOD

Large corporations have benefited greatly from this quantitative, direct cause-and-effect standard of reality/ proof and consequently now dominate our lives. In our courts of law, it commonly enables them to plead ignorance of potential defect or consequence while marketing a new product and if things go wrong, they aggressively challenge on the grounds of 'insufficient proof' (no direct, measurable linkage). Some corporate defendants simply outspend and bankrupt their opponents in court, even if their legal position in inferior…. Just drag it out!

Amongst the most powerful and legally aggressive corporations is Monsanto, which has manufactured some of the most toxic chemicals humanity has encountered, like Agent Orange, dioxin and PCBs, which The Environmental Protection Agency (EPA) classifies as 'probable carcinogens'. Monsanto is currently positioning itself as an 'agricultural company', prominent in the genetic modification of seeds and in bovine growth hormones (BGH). Both of these immensely profitable endeavours are also controversial and have engendered significant legal actions, which Monsanto has predictably fought with all of its massive resources, including intimidating Pinkerton detectives, PR campaigns, and an unlimited legal budget. Its massive advertising spending also makes most media corporations think twice about delving too deeply into its affairs.

The end result is that corporations can routinely avoid paying the real social costs of their activities, which include general environmental damage and 'difficult to prove', personal injury. Their profits consequently soar, which investors like and support. The eventual cost is borne by individuals' quality of life and sometimes by life itself. Often government has to step in to clean up the mess and injuries that corporations cause, but that too falls unto the shoulders of individuals, who finance the government's activities through taxation. So when you see all those great, cheap deals or your investments soaring, give a second thought to what the real costs might be and who is paying! If we paid the true price of our consumption, perhaps we would not consume and waste so much. We would be more encouraged to look into sustainability and equality.

Many of our current injustices and harmful practices would be remedied if individuals and institutions acknowledged as 'hard-headed reality', the fact of multiple and subtle cause-and-effect, which results in a vertical, 'both-and' rather than 'either-or' reality. It would completely transform our world, even if we retain the trappings of our present economic and legal systems.

Since this is a book about the Dao or Way of Cooking, it is not appropriate to go into detailed, comprehensive, ecological 'best practices', which would include transportation, house construction, power useage, power lines, household cleaners, clothing, beauty products, cell phones, radio waves and more. Hereunder, we would like to mention just a few important, food-related ecological issues.

Water

Water is one of the fundamental necessities for life, together with air and sun. We can live only a few days without water; 70% of the human body consists of water; all our food production depends on water. There are two aspects of water which are coming into prominence and which deserve our attention - purity and availability.

Even in the most developed countries, potable water is a veritable soup of many dozens of contaminants. It is often far worse in poorer countries, which routinely become the dumping grounds for waste from the richer countries. In addition to age-old microbial contaminants, from human and animal feces and parasites, we now have many new kinds of toxins, which are the result of our consumer, technology driven civilization. Synthetic organic contaminants include chemicals, largely from pesticides and herbicides; radiological contaminants are of course, radioactive; inorganic contaminants include asbestos, lead, fluoride, arsenic, cyanide, mercury and more; hormonal contaminants result from the hormones we ingest and expel; disinfectants like chlorine, which is itself a contaminant, react chemically with other substances. In addition to all of these, are the unknown effects of how genetic modification (GMOs) will add to the volatile brew of contaminants we have already concocted.

Growing awareness about water as a vital part of health maintenance and widespread concern about water quality have been used by global companies like Coca Cola (Dasani) and Pepsi (Aquafina) to market bottled water on a massive scale. The global rate of bottled water consumption doubled between 1997 and 2005 and its growth is expected to continue as in the past.

Although water consumption is positive for health purposes, especially if it replaces sugared pop, the bottled water industry has several drawbacks. It takes energy to manufacture the plastic bottles and to transport them; the manufacturing process of 1 litre of bottled water requires between 3 to 6 litres of water; although the plastic bottles are generally recyclable, it is estimated about 80% of them end up in landfills; there is evidence that over time, the plastic bottles leach chemicals like antimony into the water; the extraction of water may negatively impact local water sources. Remember that many of these criticisms also apply to other plastic-bottled drinks.

Most people in North America drink either tap or bottled water and the quality standards are about the same for both. Since about 25% of bottled water sold in the USA (including Dasani and Aquafina) comes from municipal tap water, a cheaper, healthier and more environmentally-friendly alternative may be tap water in refillable glass or stainless steel containers. Well and spring water may be stored in larger, preferable non-plastic containers.

Reverse osmosis and distillation are generally regarded as the systems which remove the most from water, including natural minerals. The downside of these systems, apart from the mineral extraction, is that osmosis wastes water and distillation uses a lot of power. Simpler and cheaper filtration systems like Brita may make your water taste better and take out some contaminants, but not all. Of course, if we as a society made it a priority to take much more care of what is dumped into our waterways, oceans and soil, most contaminants would not enter into the water cycle in the first place.

Although water shortage is not uppermost in most people's minds, it very much concerns the increasing numbers of those suffering from droughts (often due to global climate change), and the experts studying water and climate. Many predict that in terms of global demand, water will be the new 'oil', except much more so, since it is so vital and immediate to survival. At that point in time, it will not only be of scientific concern, but economic and political as well. Imagine a scenario wherein there is chronic drought and a great river which runs through several countries (perhaps possessing nuclear weapons of various ilk), is dammed up by the country where the river originates.

In terms of fresh, potable water, Canada will be an increasingly influential global player, if we do not in the meanwhile give away our control of this most precious resource. Canada, with a relatively small population, has between 5 ½ to 20 per cent of the world's supply, depending on how "fresh water" is defined. By any measure, Canada's per capita fresh water resources are amongst the highest in the world.

Unfortunately, all this water abundance seems to have made Canadians complacent. The average Canadian does not seemed too concerned about the control of water (or perhaps does not express her or his concern), although the issue is raised from time to time in the media. Despite our green self-image, Canadians' wasteful, daily per capita consumption of water is the second highest in the world (behind the Americans) at 350 litres. The average global citizen uses between 20 and 40 litres of water a day for both drinking and sanitation, which means the average Canadian uses 10 times as much! It is not hard to cut down on water consumption. We just have to care and be more aware.

Even as Canadians take their water blessings for granted, the rest of the world and especially the USA are setting their sights on Canadian water.

EXTERNAL ECOLOGY AND FOOD

Pressure is already being applied through the General Agreement on Tariffs and Trade (GATT) and the North American Free Trade Agreement (NAFTA). The crucial question to be resolved in these treaties is whether water is a 'vital resource' like the air we breathe, or a 'commodity', like any other which should be freely traded. If a precedent is set one way or the other, it may tilt the legal balance. Consider that the current, internationally accepted legal precedent that you can patent life (more specifically genes) originates from a United States Patent Office's (probably mistaken) interpretation of their Supreme Court rulings. At present 'bulk' water sales of water are not allowed in Canada although entrepreneurs are forever probing and pushing. Why not sell a commodity for which you are paying very little or nothing? A permit was issued to Nova Group, a Sault Ste. Marie company, allowing it to ship up to 600 million litres of Lake Superior water to Asia by 2002, but was withdrawn because of public reaction. Entrepreneur Gerry White wants to sell bulk water from pristine Gisborne Lake in Newfoundland and had the support of local mayor Frizzard of Grand Le Pierre as well as Roger Grimes, Premier of Newfoundland. There seems to be a strategy here - trumpet the well-being and livelihood of 'locals' to fight the 'big, bad' federal government. The strategy of downloading or shuffling this issue may actually work if Canadians remain complacent. Ironically, the fact that we are presently selling millions of individual bottles of water (which is allowed) is de facto bulk sale of water. This bottled water is being taken from Canada's aquifers and from its lakes, incidentally depleting resources available to the average Canadian.

Considering that the bulk sale of Canadian water impacts both its economy and sovereignty, it is mightily suspicious that this seemingly important issue has disappeared from the federal agenda. The only national Canadian political parties protesting are the minority NDP and Green Party. Is it possible that negotiation and pressure is taking place behind closed doors? The Harper Conservative (presently minority) government is pushing ahead with the 'Security and Prosperity Partnership of North America' (SPP) without any public input. This initiative between the executive powers of the USA, Canada and

Mexico, together with the most powerful corporate North American CEOs, is beyond the review of the elected bodies of the countries involved. Their agenda is not made public but likely includes access to Canadian water and oil, greater economic integration and the ability of American military forces to operate in Canada and Mexico.

Canadian NDP MP Peter Julian has alleged that SPP meetings have focused on the possibility of bulk-water sales and diversions of fresh water from Canada to the USA. The NDP claims it has obtained a 'concept paper' prepared by a U.S. think-tank involved in the SPP - the Washington, D.C.-based Centre for Strategic & International Studies. The paper emphasizes Canada's relative abundance of fresh water in North America and proposes rewriting trans-boundary water management agreements for the continent. Julian believes the federal Conservatives and Liberals plan to go along with the SPP, which would allow "not just bulk-water exports, but a move to water diversions, which will have a profound and irreversible impact on Canada's environment".

Foremost among those who have long been leading the fight for water sustainability and justice is Maude Barlow, National Chairperson of the Council of Canadians. In October 2008, she was appointed Senior Advisor on Water Issues to the President of the United Nations General Assembly. She is the author of *Blue Covenant: The Global Water Crisis and the Coming Battle for the Right to Water* and *Too Close for Comfort: Canada's Future within Fortress North America.*

Vegetarianism
One of the healthiest changes individuals can make, both for themselves and for the planet, is to switch to a more vegetarian way of eating or to become vegetarian altogether. It can be done right now and it will even save you money! Eating habits are just that – habits. Our present factory farming methods with its emphasis on cheap, fast foods are a relatively recent phenomenon. Even though animal products are part of most traditional diets, they were never consumed in the quantities to which we have become accustomed.

EXTERNAL ECOLOGY AND FOOD

A growing number of people, variously called 'environmental vegetarians' or 'economic vegetarians', are changing their way of eating as their contribution to conserving scarce resources and promoting environmental sustainability. It takes much more land (5-7 times at least), water and energy to produce animal protein rather than vegetable protein. It is estimated that every pound of feedlot beef requires 7 lbs. of grain and 2400 gallons of water, not to mention energy costs.

American consumption of meat is the highest in the world, averaging over 260 lbs. of meat a year per person (imagine that piled on your table!), which is 1.5 times higher than consumption in the industrial world and 3 times that of the East Asia. "If all the grain currently fed to livestock in the United States were consumed directly by people, the number of people who could be fed would be nearly 800 million", says David Pimentel, Professor of Ecology in Cornell University's College of Agriculture and Life Sciences. He estimates that if those grains were exported, it would boost the U.S. trade balance by $80 billion a year.

Ironically, America's successful exportation of its popular culture and Free Market capitalist ideology means that the rest of the world now wants to consume and eat like America, including countries with enormous populations like India and China. Who can blame them!? Unfortunately, it is likely that the USA and the rest of the developed world will do precisely that….watch for the blame game!

Even after meat is consumed, it requires resources. Sandra Postel (a leading authority on international freshwater issues) and Amy Vickers in 'State of the World 2004' advise: "With its high meat content, the average U.S. diet requires 5.4 cubic metres of water per person per day - twice as much as an equally nutritious vegetarian diet".

In addition to consuming large quantities of scarce resources, intensive livestock farming degrades and pollutes the environment… to a far greater extent than just crops. Trees absorb carbon dioxide (a major contributor to global warming), so when whole forests are cleared, not only is this valuable absorption capacity lost, but the burnt and rotting materials actually release additional carbon dioxide. Without a covering, soil erodes and is washed or blown away, silting up waterways, causing mudslides and in extreme circumstances, creating deserts. The clearing of forests also accelerates the extinction of species, one half of which resides in our forests.

Unlike vegetables, animals fart, excrete and actively interact with human beings. As ridiculous as it might seem, this mass animal flatulence results in significant methane emissions, which impact global warming. In intensive animal farming, vast lakes of excrement (laced with chemicals and hormones) are created and often leach into our waterways. Every pound of marketable beef generates 40 lbs. of excrement.

Historically, many disease and infections (called zoonosis or zoonoses in the plural) affecting humans have arisen from their interactions with animals. Zoonosis is now becoming quite significant because of increasing human manipulation of animals and intensive, factory farming methods. In addition, modern transportation enables someone contracting an unusual disease or infection in the remotest corner of the planet to hop on a plane and within hours be in the middle of a major city... transmitting it. Examples of zoonosis include AIDs, SARs, anthrax, Mad Cow Disease, rabies, salmonella, E.coli, parasites, listeriosis, and the ebola virus.

The intensive 'factory farming' of animals has helped recruit many new vegetarians concerned both about cruelty to animals and how meat produced under those conditions might affect human health. Typically, animals are kept in confined, overcrowded conditions, unable to move much, if at all. They are often given growth hormones or have been bred to produce flesh as fast as possible, which can lead to deformities. Because of the dirty, overcrowded, stressful conditions, animals are commonly treated with drugs (often antibiotics) to help keep them alive. Transportation to slaughter can mean many hours crammed together like sardines. Although stunning before slaughter is recommended, it is not always performed or the stunning may not work. Chickens are commonly hung by their feet on conveyor belts on their way to having their heads severed. The meat products often contain traces of feces resulting from the slaughtering and processing.

Valuing Our Food

"You are what you eat" is a saying that is true at many different levels. It seems most people do not think much about where their food comes from, assured by the tidy, cheerful packaging and shiny supermarket counters and shelves.

In Traditional Chinese Medicine (TCM), food is regarded as an important part of herbal medicine and essential health. We need a balanced diet of different food groups, preferably grown organically in a healthy environment and adapted to our specific constitution and life circumstances. All forms of life are manifestation of Qi or energy and that includes our food, which we take into ourselves. Thus it is important what nutrients and additives go into that food, how that food lives (including animals), how it is harvested, how it is prepared and how it is cooked for our consumption and celebration.

As human beings, nothing is more essential to basic survival than air, water and food. In times of inflated prosperity and conspicuous spending, these may seem to be trivial. However, in terms of our very survival, they are paramount. We are presently undervaluing the essentials of life. Spending more money to improve the quality of air, water and food, may in the short term seem too costly, but we pay in the long term in terms of our health and quality of life. When we eventually get 'sick', how much do we spend on drugs, medical procedures and hospitalization?

Farmers and consumers are proving that organic, low intensity farming using traditional methods is economically viable and better for the environment (and therefore for us). By eating more, fresh, local, organic produce, we can cut down on transportation costs, improve the quality of our food and lessen the loss of bio-diversity (e.g. hundreds of millions of people eating just two or three varieties of apples or pears). We can also cut costs and at the same time reduce garbage by reducing packaging.

Encouraging broad-based local production, in all countries, will also add stability to our global food systems. At present, small (mostly tropical) countries are encouraged to specialize in export oriented 'cash crops' like coffee, cotton, bananas, oranges etc. If the market tumbles, those countries can neither grow the food to sustain their populations nor afford to import food. Our attitude to food, being so fundamental, reflects our broader attitudes to life. The more aware we are of our interconnections and the more we value and take care of what we have, the healthier (in its widest and most profound sense), we will become.

Our attitude to food and eating, since they are so fundamental, reflects broader attitudes to life generally. If we take more care and show greater appreciation about how and why we eat, our lives will be enriched both individually and collectively.

Food as Healing

In the previous section, we have been discussing the Value of Food mostly in terms of preventative health care and environmental sustainability. However, there have been innumerable, often dramatic, cases featuring people who have survived very serious illnesses mainly through changing what they eat. Hereunder are just two such examples of food as medicine.

The first example is very close to home - Nicola's father, Derek. Derek, Margaret and their young toddlers, Chris and Nicola, immigrated to Canada from England in 1966. Derek was a regular guy (bloke) who liked red meat, "chips", junk food, white bread, sugar, pubs and partying. Derek was also a smoker but stopped just before coming to Canada. He

EXTERNAL ECOLOGY AND FOOD

and Margaret worked hard to build a new life initially in Toronto and then Holland Landing, just north of Newmarket. About 15 years later (circa 1981), thanks to the prodding of a precocious and spirited teenage daughter, Derek began to pay attention to his diet. He stopped eating red meat and chicken and drastically cut down on sugar and processed food. He and Margaret became active members of the Vegetarian Society.

In 1995, at the age of sixty-five, Derek finally retired. However, within months of his retirement, in a seemingly cruel Twist of Fate, Derek discovered he had prostate cancer, which had already metastasized. His life expectancy was estimated at 5 years maximum. Instead of meekly accepting this prediction, Derek was determined to do whatever he could to live as long as possible. In addition to conventional surgery and radiation, Derek focused on food as a way to try to improve his health. He completely gave up alcohol and coffee, and further reduced his intake of carbohydrates and sweeteners. He joined a local, prostate cancer support group and positively channeled his energies into educating people about prostate cancer.

Fast forward to 2009. Approaching the age of 79, Derek has outlasted his death prediction by at least 9 years, has become a celebrated, national 'poster boy' for prostate cancer survival, and is being invited to speak all across Canada. He is still very physically active, undertaking all sorts of demanding building and maintenance projects at Harmony Dawn and elsewhere. Over the last five years, he has been a regular participant at our Harmony Dawn cooking and meditation workshops, where he is proud to demonstrate all the vegetarian culinary skills and knowledge he has accumulated over the years as well as his willingness to continually learn and explore.

The second example of food as healing concerns Dr. David Servan-Schreiber, considerably more famous and formally educated than Derek Lawrence, but no more tenacious or convinced of the healing power of food.

Servan-Schreiber was and is an eminent medical establishment insider - physician, researcher, and director of the Center for Integrative Medicine at the University of Pittsburg. His specialization is psychiatry and the functioning of the brain. He was ambitious, young, healthy and athletic, when at the age of thirty-one, during one of his own studies on brain tumours, he was shocked to discover that he himself had a serious brain tumour. He later commented on how quickly his colleagues' perception of him changed - no more the powerful, knowledgeable Doctor, but a relatively powerless, victim-like Patient. After conventional medical treatment, his cancer went into remission.

David acknowledged that he subsequently did nothing to really change the "terrain" of his life, hoping and trusting that everything would be all right. He became complacent and even cocky, having "beaten" cancer. His life became busier and more stressful, since he now had a son to look after in addition to all his professional commitments. His regular, hurried lunch at that time was chile con carne, a bagel and a can of coke, which in hindsight he described as "an explosive combination of white flour, sugar, together with animal fats loaded with omega-6s, hormones, and environmental toxins"... extremely fertile ground for cancer. Just a few years after his initial bout with cancer, it reappeared in the very same spot in his brain.

The return of cancer was a wake-up call to Servan-Schreiber and convinced him that he had to make major changes in his life in order to survive it. However, when he asked his oncologist for advice, he was told, "There is nothing special you can do. Lead your life normally. We'll do MRI scans at regular intervals....Do what you like. It can't do you any harm. But we don't have any scientific evidence that any of these approaches can prevent a relapse".

Undeterred, he used his considerable research skills to hunt out anything that might help him live longer, examining not only conventional medicine, but non-conventional as well, including Oriental medicine. He eventually found persuasive evidence that cancer patients who ate

External Ecology and Food

better and learned to live in harmony with their bodies and minds, lived two to three times longer than those in a similar condition who did nothing.

He was particularly struck by the work of Dr. Dean Ornish, who in 2005 published the results of a ground-breaking study in oncology. Ninety-three men with early-stage prostate cancer choose not to undergo surgery for one year, but simply to remain under the close surveillance of their oncologists. They were divided into two groups of even numbers by drawing lots. The control group was monitored by having their PSA (prostate specific antigen) levels regularly tested but otherwise did nothing special.

For the second group, Dr. Ornish set up a special program of physical and mental health. This included a vegetarian diet with supplements, 30 minutes of walking 6 days a week, 1 hour per week in a support group with other patients in the same program and practice in stress management (yoga movements, breathing exercises, mental imagery or progressive relaxation).

At the end of the year, the results were dramatic. Of the control group, 6 (over 12%) saw their cancer worsen and underwent treatment; the PSA level of the group increased on average by 6% which suggested that their tumors were growing. In the second group with the lifestyle changes, none required treatment; the average PSA level decreased by 4%; their blood was 7 times more capable of inhibiting the growth of cancerous cells than those in the control group.

Here in a brutally short paragraph, are the major findings of Servan-Schreiber best-selling and highly praised book, Anticancer: A new Way of Life, published in 2007. Certain foods can act like anticancer medications, while others, like sugar, can actually promote cancer. The dynamics of the mind and emotions can similarly inhibit or promote cancer. The fitness of the physical body can help fight cancer. When *Anticancer* was published, David was 14 years cancer free, following the advice he advocated in his book, and beating the odds.

Servan-Schreiber's discoveries point towards the validity of much of what we have been proposing and practicing at Harmony Dawn - the multi-level interconnection of our internal and external environments.

Welcome To The Harmony Dawn Kitchen

I have learned a great deal about how people approach food and cooking from the feedback I get from guests attending the retreat and also from teaching my cooking workshops. For the most part, the one thing everyone seems to have in common is the actual love of food and eating. Cooking, well that is another matter. Time constraints, busy lives, children and demanding jobs all take a toll. Most people are simply too tired, but it isn't without trying or wanting to. I often hear "How can I prepare nutritious food like yours without it taking all day?" or "I feel so good eating this way but how can I get all the nutrients from a vegetarian diet?" or the hardest one, "How do I get my kids and husband on board?"

One thing I try to encourage in my workshops is a sense of community. It's about getting everyone in the family involved in food preparation; making it an important and integral part of the day, as important as working or going to school. I feel that we as a society have lost our connection to food and the earth, so involvement is a key factor in re-establishing that link and taking more control over our health and lives.

If you live alone, it is important to value and nurture yourself through cooking. I realize that most recipes are designed for more than one person and with that in mind I have purposefully created a lot of stir fries, noodle and rice bowls, fast and simple soups. With a little bit of knowledge and forethought, a single diner (or a family) can transform their weekly dining experience. For example, left-over rice can be made into in a burger for lunch and then into porridge; left-over beans from a salad can be thrown into a quick soothing broth, or put on a toasted baguette.

I encouraged and welcomed feedback from *The Dao of Harmony Dawn Cooking* and have tried to incorporate all the suggestions in this book. You will find information pages on soy, tempeh, seitan, legumes, rice and noodle bowls, helpful cooking tips, eco tips about the environment, a glossary and a comprehensive index - all written to aid your cooking journey. As with my first book, *Eco Harmony Dawn Cooking* is comprised primarily of vegetarian and vegan recipes with just a few sustainable fish recipes. You will find that all of the recipes are relatively low in fat, sodium and sweeteners, including the Desserts chapter, and all are made using the finest of unrefined natural ingredients available.

There are about 180 recipes in *Eco Harmony Dawn Cooking*, ranging in skill from simple to more elaborate. Read through the recipes and start with something you feel you can tackle and work up from there as your confidence grows. Remember cooking is actually a lot of fun and a creative expression of our true nature. So play with the recipes, add a smidge of something here or a dash there and remember never ever panic. Sometimes my best recipes were born out of an error, a miscalculation or changing an ingredient due to an allergy. You never know what can happen and where inspiration will come from. Have fun!

Nicola, Andy, Margaret & Derek Lawrence

Welcome To The Harmony Dawn Kitchen

How to Use My Book

All the recipes in *Eco Harmony Dawn Cooking* are made using organic, local and sustainable ingredients as much as is practical. Due to space constraints, the word "organic" does not appear beside individual items. All of the ingredients and staples you will need can be found in most supermarkets, Asian markets, specialty markets or natural/health food stores.

There are helpful hints scattered throughout the book to help you with an ingredient or technique. Individual recipes will indicate where you can find an ingredient if it is unusual. Please refer to the glossary for information on specific items and general cooking terms like roasting garlic and peppers, making pureed date sugar, flax eggs etc.

There are many vegan recipes in this book and they are clearly marked on the top of each recipe. Vegan means they do not use ingredients derived from animals such as butter, milk and milk products, animal meats and honey. I have indicated appropriate substitutions where applicable.

A great way to learn about new and unfamiliar ingredients is to go into your neighborhood health food store or the Bulk Barn and mosey around and ask for assistance. Most major health food stores actually give tours and discussions for a minimal fee or are willing to answer your questions over the phone. Help is never that far away.

Food Storage

Studies have shown that one third of all food purschased in North America is discarded because of poor storage. Every year this costs the average family several hundred dollars and also represents significant wasteage of scarce resources - land, water, energy and labour.

Fruits and Vegetables

Proper storage increases the shelf life of food and also aides in preventing the growth of bacteria and unwanted germs. Most vegetables should be stored in the refrigerator with the exception of onions, garlic, potatoes, sweet potatoes and squashes which should be stored in a cool dark place. Tomatoes are fine on the counter and will become pulpy if put in the refrigerator. Leafy greens keep fresher when washed, drained and then wrapped in a towel stored in a bag or container in the refrigerator. All other vegetables are best washed prior to using. Most fruit including avocados are best stored at room temperature until ripe and then store in the refrigerator. Exceptions to this are all berries, apples, grapes, pineapple and kiwis which should be stored in the refrigerator. Herbs and berries should only be washed before you intend to use them as they will go off quickly. To reduce fruit flies and their eggs, wash all fruit in a vegetable wash when you bring them home from the store, particularly in warm humid months.

The recipes in this book require all root vegetables to be peeled. This includes carrots, potatoes, sweet potatoes, beets and squashes.

Dry Storage Goods

Check dates on all purchased goods for expiration and how best to store. Flours, grains and nuts should be kept in a cool, dark place, ideally a fridge or freezer as they can go rancid very quickly given the right circumstances. Temperature and humidity all play a key role. Dried spices like to be in a dark place and anything red like chili pepper, paprika, cayenne and curry powder, loose their potency quicker if not stored in the fridge.

Storing food in glass containers/jars is preferable to plastic containers for many reasons. Research has found that plastic can leach toxins into our foods if food is stored improperly. Plastics are crowding our landfills, polluting our countryside and poisoning us so they are considered an unsustainable storage choice. Fortunately you can now purchase tempered glass storage containers in a range of shapes and sizes. They stack well and can be used from stove to freezer and vice versa. Save your glass jars from purchased goods and recycle them because they are great for leftovers, herbs etc.

Welcome To The Harmony Dawn Kitchen

A helpful addition to my kitchen has been the Food Saver system. It suctions out air (which encourages bacteria) and increases the shelf life of dry goods such as granola, nuts and seeds and also for wet goods such as prepared legumes and lentils. Unfortunately it uses plastic bags so I do use it sparingly and only when the temperature is fluctuating.

Organics

There are many reasons to buy organic produce and goods. First and foremost, they taste better; secondly, they do not contain toxic pesticides that create disease in our bodies. Organic farming uses natural and healthy farming methods such as compost and beneficial insects, which enhance the soil rather than deplete it. A vast majority of organic farms are small and independently owned. In buying their produce you are supporting their efforts and their dedication to helping your health and the health of the planet.

Fruits and vegetables do not come with labels telling you what has been sprayed on them or how they have been grown. It is easy to think "what's the difference?" when you are shopping. Health Canada imposes strict standards that organic farming must meet to be labeled "organic". For example the produce must be grown without the use of chemical fertilizers, herbicides, pesticides, fumigants and toxins. They also prohibit the use of antibiotics, growth hormones, steroids, artificial colours and artificial fragrances. If you purchase packaged non organic goods, get in the habit of scrutinizing the labels and then compare them with a similar organic product to see the differences. If you can't pronounce or spell the ingredient, then chances are it's not very good for you.

If you can't afford to go all organic, here is a list of the current top 12 best and worst in order of their toxicity. Check www.thedailygreen.com for regular updates and for more information.

Worst	Best
Peaches	Onion

Apples	Avocado
Bell peppers	Sweet corn
Celery	Pineapple
Nectarines	Mango
Strawberries	Asparagus
Cherries	Sweet Peas
Kale	Kiwi
Lettuce	Cabbage
Grapes (imported)	Eggplant
Carrot	Papaya
Pear	Watermelon
Potatoes	Broccoli

Stocking the Pantry

The following list incorporates what you will need to make all the recipes in *Eco Harmony Dawn Cooking*. Please do not let it intimidate you if you are unfamiliar with any of them and don't run out and buy everything. Simply start by using a few basic items and then branch out from there as your confidence grows and your skills develop.

Baking

There are many different types of flours available, but for the purpose of this book, a simple selection will suffice (all organic) - unbleached all-purpose, whole wheat bread and pastry, spelt, rye, buckwheat, potato, brown rice and chick pea flour.

Additional baking ingredients are as follows: baking soda, non aluminum baking powder, active dry yeast, Dutch cocoa powder, carob powder, semi sweet baking chocolate or chocolate chips, carob chips, pure extracts - vanilla, almond, mint, coconut, orange and lemon.

Grains

Brown rice, Thai black rice, wild rice, basmati, millet, barley, quinoa, bulgur, couscous, oats, wheat bran, wheat germ and cornmeal

Welcome To The Harmony Dawn Kitchen

Dried Lentils, Legumes and Peas
Navy, great northern, cannellini, black, kidney, adzuki, lentils-red, brown, green, black, Le Puy, split peas- green and yellow, chick peas, black eyed peas

Sweeteners
Honey, maple syrup, brown rice syrup, Sucanat, unrefined fine cane sugar, molasses, dates, applesauce

Condiments and Seasonings
Salts: Himalayan, coarse and fine sea, finishing salts, vegetable salt, tamari, Bragg all purpose seasoning, extra old aged organic soy sauce, soy sauce, kecap manis, miso-light and dark, Mirin, hoisin sauce, sambal oelek, chili oil, black bean sauce, umeboshi paste, chili sauce, chipotles in adobo, Dijon mustard, hot mustard, mayonnaise, nayonnaise, nutritional yeast, Worcestershire sauce, olives-black, green, kalamata, vegetable stock cubes-non msg (monosodium glutamate), kaffir lime leaves, wood ears, dried shiitake mushrooms, dried porcini mushrooms

Oil and Vinegar
Oils: cold pressed extra virgin olive, toasted sesame, safflower, canola, vegetable, grape seed, walnut, vegetable spray oil, peanut, flax seed
Vinegars: aged balsamic-red and white, white wine, red wine, cider, sherry, tarragon, rosemary, rice wine-brown and white, umeboshi, fig, raspberry

Thickeners
Tahini, kudzu, arrowroot, tapioca, agar

Dried fruits
Thompson's raisins, sultanas, currants, cranberries, blueberries, apricots, dates

Nuts and Seeds
All unsalted: almonds, pecans, walnuts, cashews, coconut, hazelnuts, peanuts, pine nuts, brazil, sunflower seeds, pumpkin seeds, flax seeds-

dark and light, white and black sesame seeds, peanut butter, almond butter, tahini-sesame seed butter, cashew butter

Sea Vegetables
Dulse, Arame, Hijiki, Nori, Kombu

Noodles and Pasta
Egg, Udon, Pad Thai, brown rice noodles, kamut pasta, brown rice pasta, small lentil pasta

Dried Herbs and Spices
Storage life should be checked periodically as they lose their potency after a few months.

Basil, oregano, rosemary, paprika, sweet paprika, chili powder, bay leaves, dill, tarragon, coriander seeds and powder, cumin seeds and powder, garam masala, dried chili flakes, peppercorns-black and Sichuan, curry powder, cayenne, turmeric, sage, marjoram, thyme, herbes de Provence, mustard powder, onion and garlic powder, Chinese 5 spice powder, cinnamon, nutmeg, cardamom, allspice, cloves, dried ginger, mace, anise seeds

Soy
Tempeh and tofu, miso paste

Prepared Foods
Pesto sauce, tomato sauce, canned tomatoes, tomato paste, canned beans, frozen puff pastry, whole wheat pitas, tortilla wraps

Dairy and such
Butter, buttermilk, cow's milk, soy milk, almond milk, rice milk, yogurt, organic or free range eggs, parmesan cheese, Monterey Jack cheese, cheddar cheese, mozzarella cheese

Welcome To The Harmony Dawn Kitchen

Equipment Pantry
This is a list of the most useful equipment I have in my kitchen. It is not necessary to have them all and certainly some items are more costly than others but start slow and build as your confidence and skill level grows.

Electrical Gadgets
I live in an environmentally off grid house and I would love to tell you that I don't own any electrical gadgets in my kitchen. But that simply isn't true. I could not work without my food processor, immersion hand blender or Magic Bullet mini chopper.

I would recommend you purchase a food processor if you have the room as they are an indispensable item for cutting, pureeing, slicing, pulverizing, whipping, making bread dough and pastry. They make an arduous chopping task fun and fast. Immersion hand blenders are awesome because you can insert them directly into your soup pot or for making smoothies. My Magic Bullet mini chopper is perfect for small jobs like grinding spices, nuts and small amounts of garlic and ginger. It has a storage seal so you can prepare ahead of time and keep in the fridge until you need.

A counter top toaster oven is ideal for the small jobs that don't require a whole oven and saves on power. A pressure cooker is a time and energy saver but also is a good method of cooking because it utilizes steam, sealing in all the nutrients.

Additional item: a rice cooker-they can range in size for 2 people to 20; Crock-Pot slow cooker-ideal for overnight breakfast grains or for making stews while you are at work; stand mixer (luxury item) for baking, whipping and breads; dehydrator for long term food storage. Mine is built into my oven but you can purchase electric ones. A juicer and a blender come in handy if you like fresh juices and smoothies. Lastly my Food Saver - this is the ultimate in food storage systems and is new to my kitchen. It suctions out all the air and air is what encourages bacteria, so your food is preserved longer. It also prevents freezer burn.

Knives
Good knives will last you for years especially with proper care. Invest in one knife at a time. When purchasing a knife, feel it in your hand - the weight of it, the size and ultimately what you are using it for. I find my 8 inch and 6 inch Wustof chef's knives are indispensable and I use them for everything. A few smaller paring knives fill in the gaps and perform well for small jobs. Invest in a good sharpening tool and sharpen regularly, a dull knife is far more dangerous than a sharp knife.

Baking Equipment
Stainless steel mixing bowls of various sizes, glass bowls, good spatulas, measuring spoons and cups for dry ingredients, liquid measures, wire whisk, rolling pin and wooden mixing spoons.

Baking sheets are versatile and can be used for different dishes ranging from pizza to cookies and they come in all different sizes. Muffin tins, mini muffin tins, bread/loaf pans, cake pans of varying sizes, square and round, pie plates, cheesecake pans with removable bottoms, flan pan, parchment paper, cooling racks, casserole dish and a deep dish pan.

Pots and Pans
This is entirely a matter of choice and what works for you. It isn't necessary to go to the expense of buying a large elaborate set if you are not going to use them. I have a good quality stainless steel set of 4 pots in different sizes and large stock pot for making soups and stews. They have heavy duty handles and thick bottoms which prevent burning and distribute heat evenly. Also helpful is a stainless steel skillet that can go from stove top to oven. A double boiler is handy for steaming and for cooking foods that cannot take direct heat. I tend to stay away from Teflon pans as I am unsure of their safety.

Additional items: a stove top grill pan, crepe or omelette pan, wok, enamel coated Dutch oven and a roasting pan.

Welcome To The Harmony Dawn Kitchen

Miscellaneous

Wooden cutting boards, colanders, strainers, vegetable peelers, a metal stand grater, a kitchen rasp-small flat grater for citrus, citrus reamer-small hand held wooden device for extracting juice, ladle, timer, salad spinner funnel, potato masher, mortar and pestle and electric spice grinder.

Menu Balancing and Planning

Vegetarian meal planning offers much more variety and creativity than the traditional "meat and two vegetables". Drawing on the vast repertoire of global cuisine, you will be building your meals around protein sources (such as soy, tempeh, nuts and wheat gluten), and balancing it with carbohydrates (rice, grains, pasta, and breads), fresh fruit and vegetables. Whole foods feed your body with nurturing vitamins, minerals and fuel without overloading your system with fat and sodium.

One of the most frequent questions I get asked is, "How will I get enough protein if I am not eating meat?" Most people eat too much protein, largely as a result of a diet heavy with meat and dairy products which are also high in fat. Women need about 50 grams of protein a day and men about 63 grams. The average person easily consumes these amounts without much thought.

Planning your meals in advance will make it easier to have a balanced diet plan and also can save time by reducing your shopping trips.

I include hereunder some basic information on protein, carbohydrates and fiber and how to incorporate them together to make a complete meal.

Proteins

Protein is what gives structure to all living things. Even the tiniest microbe is composed of protein. Proteins are composed of combinations of 22 amino acids. When protein is consumed, the body breaks it down into amino acids. The body can manufacture most of them but there are

8 that are considered essential to include in our diets because the body does not manufacture them.

"Complete proteins" contain all 8 essential amino acids. They are found in meat, fish, fowl, eggs, wheat germ, soy and dairy products. In "partially complete proteins", most of the necessary amino acids are present, but one or two are missing. Foods that provide this type of protein are legumes, (beans and peas) nuts, seeds, brown rice, whole grains, and brewer's yeast. A third group "incomplete proteins", contain few amino acids. Fruit, corn and vegetables fit into this group.

The body can properly utilize the incomplete and partially complete proteins only if all eight essential amino acids are ingested at, or about the same time. This means that menus may be planned so that foods that are sources of some but not all of the essential amino acids are combined into complete proteins. Thus meat, fish and poultry are not the only sources of complete protein foods. In fact, because of their high fat content - as well as antibiotics and other chemicals - most of those foods should be eaten in moderation.

This is where combining in menu planning comes in. Cereal, toast, beans and rice are not adequate proteins when eaten separately. To make a complete protein combine:

Lentils/Peas	with	brown rice, corn, nuts, seeds, or wheat
Brown rice	with	legumes, nuts, seeds, wheat
Legumes	with	wheat, corn, oats, barley, sesame and sunflower seeds
Cereal	with	milk and whole wheat toast

In order to get a variety of protein (amino acids) in your diet you can add seeds and nuts, or use nut butters instead of butter.

Sunflower seeds contain 24 percent protein of a quality almost equal to meat. They are a good source of polyunsaturated oils, including one

Welcome To The Harmony Dawn Kitchen

believed to be important to our hearts. They contain six vitamins and six minerals, including zinc and B6, both of which are difficult to get in sufficient quantities in normal diets. If you sprout sunflower seeds, you get the added benefit of live enzymes.

Legumes (beans, peas, lentils, peanuts etc.) are superstars. They are low cost, low in saturated fats, and low in calories. They combine easily with other foods to make complete proteins. They are also rich in fiber.

Bragg Liquid Amino is a seasoning that tastes like and is a substitute for soy sauce and tamari. It contains amino acids.

Nutritional Yeast is a dietary supplement and condiment. It is a good source of protein, iron, and several B vitamins. It can be added to soup, baked with nuts and seeds, sprinkled on toast, popcorn or spaghetti.

Raw Wheat Germ is a complete protein and has an even higher concentration of minerals and vitamins than whole wheat. It is 26 percent complete, more complete than meat. It is high in fiber, B vitamins, zinc, and vitamin E. Add to cereals, breads, sauces, desserts.

Buckwheat is usually found roasted, or ground into flour. It is not a grain but a member of the rhubarb family. It contains all eight amino acids and is a good source of calcium, vitamin E, and B complex vitamins. When using buckwheat flour, it needs to be combined with glutinous flour such as whole wheat or spelt.

Carbohydrates
Carbohydrates supply the body with energy. There are two different types, simple carbohydrates, which are sugars, and complex carbohydrates, which are starches.

Natural sources of sugar that I use at the retreat centre are honey, blackstrap and unsulfured molasses, brown rice syrup, barley malt syrup, Sucanat, dates and date sugar, maple syrup, agave nectar and fresh fruit.

Other natural sources are stevia, cane syrup, turbinado sugar and beet sugar. The sugars in fruits are valuable because they are ingested more slowly than refined sugar and the fruits themselves contain important bulk fiber, which slows down digestion.

Refined sugars have minimal if any nutritional value. They provide calories (empty) and nothing else of value. They disrupt calcium levels, increase the need for vitamin B complex, decrease the body's ability to combat infection and recover from disease and surgery, and lower immune responses to infection. Refined sugar is often combined commercially with synthetic flavours and colours that contain allergens which are particularly harmful to children. Raw sugar which is naturally tawny in colour, is bleached and purified by running it through a filter of bone char, the carbon residue of superheated cattle bones.

Starches consist of grains, flours made from grains, prepared foods made from grain flours, and vegetables. They are a source of energy and complex starches (unrefined) are excellent foods. They are absorbed more slowly than sugars. Their bulk aids in digestion and elimination and decreases the risk of colon cancer. It is important to eat only unrefined whole grains. Brown rice is my favourite. Whole wheat is a substantial source of complex carbohydrates. Wheat contains iron, potassium, chromium, B vitamins, vitamin E, zinc, and small amounts of manganese and calcium.

Refined grains and flours have had the vitamins and minerals removed in the husking and bleaching processes. Combine these with refined sugar on a long term basis and you have a recipe for illness.

Fiber

Fiber is the indigestible vegetable residue from the plants that we eat, providing roughage and bulk in our diet. Fiber helps to lower blood cholesterol levels, stabilize blood sugar levels, reduce the risk of heart disease and aid in the removal of toxins and excess estrogen. It is good for digestion, helps to relieve constipation and aids in overall colon

WELCOME TO THE HARMONY DAWN KITCHEN

health. There are two types of fiber, insoluble and soluble. Insoluble fiber is found in whole grain cereals and flours, all types of bran, nuts and seeds and brown rice. Soluble fiber is found in beans, legumes, lentils, raw vegetables and fruits. Eating a combination of both on a daily basis will improve overall health.

Fruits and Vegetables
Fruits and vegetables are high in vitamins, antioxidants, minerals and above all fiber, it is important to eat a variety to maximize health benefits.

Daily Requirements
What are your recommended daily requirements of protein, carbohydrates, fiber and vegetables? A lot depends on your size and sex, whether you are an adult or a child etc. There are many resources which go into this in detail. I have included a few in the Resource section of my book. It is good to have an idea of proper portion sizes when creating your meals for the day. Numerous studies have shown people tend to eat what is put in front of them regardless of portion control. We have become accustomed to gigantic super size portions especially in fast foods. A small juice today was a large juice in 1970. Below is a simple guide on how to put together a plate.

Protein - think of a deck of cards which represents 1 serving of meat or tofu (3-4 oz or 100 grams), a ⅓ cup of beans, or 2 tablespoons of peanut butter
Complex Carbohydrates - think of a computer mouse or 1 cup of grains like rice or pasta.
Simple Carbohydrates - think of a tennis ball or ½ cup of milk products (dairy, soy or almond) or 1 fruit serving. Vegetables - think of a light bulb or ½ cup.
Fat - think of a dice or 1 tablespoon of butter, fat or salad dressing.

The Yin and Yang of Harmony Dawn Cooking
Although I described Yin Yang theory in my first book *The Dao of*

Harmony Dawn Cooking I feel it is important to briefly revisit it. Yin yang principles are not only a fundamental part my cooking philosophy, but of Harmony Dawn itself.

An integral part of macrobiotic theory is the Chinese concept of Yin and Yang – seemingly opposite yet complementary natural forces that create an orderly, balanced universe. Yin and yang are difficult to describe in Western terms, because they are energetic concepts, not tangible objects. The way yin and yang interact regulates every dimension of life from the spiritual to the physical. Nothing is exclusively yin or yang; both forces exist in all things.

Macrobiotics classifies each food as yin or yang in relation to other foods. In other words, yin and yang are relative rather than absolute concepts. Whether a food is relatively more yin or yang depends on a variety of factors, including where it was grown, its mineral and water contents, colour, texture, taste and effect on the body. Whole grains and most vegetables fall near the mid point between yin and yang, making them nourishing mainstays of the macrobiotic diet. Sugar, refined foods and stimulants like coffee and chocolate are considered highly yin, causing energy imbalances, nervousness, worry and lack of focus. Red meats, cheese and refined salt are believed to be extremely yang, producing tight muscles, congestion, and tending us towards hostility and criticism.

Macrobiotic practitioners generally design meals to produce a yin-yang balance while avoiding extremes in individual foods. Selecting more balanced foods promotes physical and mental vitality, equilibrium and a positive outlook. It also reduces craving, which is a sign of imbalance.

Yin=Acid and Yang=Alkaline

The buffet table at Harmony Dawn incorporates a balanced approach to the menu. Our bodies perform at their best in a balanced environment of Yin/acid and yang/alkaline. For example, if you are too Yin or acidic, you may not sleep well or may become prone to headaches and infections.

Welcome To The Harmony Dawn Kitchen

There may be too much lactic acid build up in your body if you are athletic. The way to bring your acid levels down is by the addition of healthy Yang/alkaline foods (listed below).

Acidity and alkalinity of the body can be measured according to your pH (potential of hydrogen) scale. The scale runs from zero to 14. A pH of 7.0 is considered neutral- neither acid nor alkaline. Anything with a pH below 7.0 is acid and anything above 7.0 is alkaline. The ideal range for the human body is between 6.0 and 6.8. The higher the pH number, the more alkaline, and the lower the number, the more acidic your body is. Purchase pH paper at your local drugstore and apply urine to the test. The paper will change colour to indicate if your system is acidic or alkaline.

Our diet should be comprised of 75 percent alkaline foods and 25 percent acidic foods. The buffet table at Harmony Dawn incorporates this balanced approach to the menu. For example Quinoa Vegetable Patties (pg. 193) is slightly acidifying on its own, but adding a large green garden salad with fresh shredded vegetables balances the meal. A brief outline of acidifying and alkalizing foods is included below.

Acidic Foods
All oils, grains, most dairy, most nuts including tahini, animal protein except eggs, pasta, beans and legumes, sugars and sweeteners, alcohol.

Alkaline Foods
All vegetables, all fruits, sea vegetables, shiitakes, umboshi, spices and seasonings such as miso, tamari, curry, cinnamon, eggs, tempeh, tofu, seeds, millet, almonds, green tea, herbal teas, apple cider vinegar and stevia. Qi gong, Tai Chi, meditation, deep breathing and yoga also help tremendously to keep the body in balance and alkaline.

Five Elements of Food Tasting
Taste and smell are the most important tools in the kitchen. They enable us to balance the flavours of the foods we are preparing and to correct

those imbalances before the food hits our tables. Flavour therefore is a mixture of taste, aroma, texture and temperature. When we eat food our mouth recognizes 5 tastes - sweet, sour, salty, bitter and savoury which is called umami in Japanese.

Common examples of the 4 basic flavours are: sweet (fruit, sugars, honey etc.), sour (citrus, acids, vinegars), salty (sodium, fish sauce, chilis, hot sauce) and bitter (tonic, Worcestershire sauce, beer). The 5th umami or savoury taste rounds out the flavours of the foods it accompanies and increases complexity. It has a taste commomly associated with meat and fermented foods. Examples of umami are seaweed, miso paste, soy sauce, tamari, shiitake mushrooms, anchovies, tomato paste and Parmesan cheese.

When you are cooking a dish, taste along the way and see what is missing or stands out too much and then use the other flavours to balance the dish. Is it too sweet or not sweet enough? Does it need a bit of salt or a dash of tamari? With a little practice you will begin to develop your skills, allowing you to be more creative in your kitchen.

Basic Kitchen Skills

Here is my list of the top 12 basic skills that I teach prior to the beginning of our Cooking for Health seasonal workshops.

1. First remember that cooking is fun and creative.
2. Wash and sterilize your hands and wear an apron to protect your clothes.
3. Clean your counters and sterilize after use with lemon juice.
4. Regardless of your skill level, read through the recipe carefully and take note of ingredients, equipment, projected time. Ask yourself, "Is this something I can do?"
5. Familiarize yourself with basic techniques like kneading, sifting, stir frying, steaming, deglazing.
6. Familiarize yourself with measurements. What quantity does a teaspoon, tablespoon or cup look like? Practice measuring with some

salt on a plate so you can "eye" it when you are cooking.

7. Learn the basic cutting techniques: mince, dice, chop, julienne, slice, shred, chiffonade.

8. There are different knives for different tasks and you need to feel comfortable when holding one. Think of it as an extension of your body and mind. If you are nervous, you will make a mistake and hurt yourself. Learning how to use a knife properly is like learning how to write.

9. Good quality knives are expensive and need to be maintained and taken care of properly. Always wash by hand and dry promptly, never dull the point, learn proper sharpening skills. If you cook a lot, you should be sharpening your knives weekly. A dull knife is more dangerous than a sharp knife.

10. A clean, tidy workspace is a happy workspace. Keep your station tidy so you don't get confused.

11. Organize your ingredients and have them ready. There is nothing worse than hunting for something when you need it NOW!

12. Mistakes are creations and this is where you learn. Have fun! Don't panic!

Tofu

Tofu (bean curd made from soybeans) has been around for thousands of years in China and Japan. It is an excellent source of calcium, protein and minerals and unlike high protein animal foods, it has an alkaline composition.

It is a multi purpose food that has the ability to absorb other flavours, making it perfect for marinating and ideal in both savoury dishes as well as sweet desserts. Tofu can be puréed, left whole, baked, grilled, sautéed or fried.

Tofu (bean curd) is basically curdled soy milk which has been separated into curds and whey. The amount of whey pressed out of the soymilk curds determines the final product. Soft tofu is great for making dips, dressings and desserts. Firm tofu has the moist texture of raw meat and is good for salads and scrambling. Extra-firm tofu is more resilient and dense; it holds its shape well and is perfect for stir-fries and steaks. Silken tofu is soft and custard like and usually comes in 10 ounce tetra packs that do not require refrigeration. Silken tofu is what I use for icings and sauces. It is also used in a popular Asian dessert called Doufuhua, which is normally served with a warm, mild sugar syrup.

Asian markets sell many types of tofu skin, which develops on the surface of the tofu. Mild and chewy, it is used as a wrapper for sweet or savoury fillings.

Freezing tofu changes its texture. The water during freezing crystallizes and when it melts you are left with a spongy, chewy meat like texture that absorbs marinades and flavours better than non frozen tofu. To freeze, drain the package of tofu first and wrap in plastic wrap or slice the tofu into steaks, placing them on a baking sheet in the freezer and freezing until firm. Then simply wrap into individual packages.

When using tofu (unfrozen), it is important to drain and press the water from the packaged tofu, with the exception of silken tofu.

THE BASIC PROTEINS & BUILDING BLOCKS

The reason for doing this is it will make the tofu firmer and with the excess water gone, it will be able to absorb marinades and spices better. To remove excess water, simply wrap the tofu in a towel and place in a colander in the sink. Place a can or something heavy on top. The excess water should drain off in about 30 minutes.

It is very important to seek out and buy organic tofu. Within the last 10 years, soybeans have become one of the most successfully genetically modified (GMO) crops in the United States with approximately 90% of all soybean crops coming from GMO plants. In 1995 Monsanto Company introduced a product called Roundup Ready soybeans containing altered DNA into the North American market place. In many countries around the world, GMO's are outlawed due to the health risks associated with them.

Tofu and all soy products contain phytoestrogens. Phytoestrogens are a group of substances with a chemical structure similar to estrogen. There are reports that suggest too much soy phytoestrogens can be harmful to women, specifically with breast cancer. On the other hand, there are reports that suggest the exact opposite is true and soy is very beneficial to health on many levels. Within the vegetarian community, tofu has been touted as a universal meat substitute and as such is overused in many vegetarian products, specifically manufactured process foods.

I believe in balance which is what my book and the retreat centre is all about. But it is important for you to understand what is happening to your food, what that food source is and its impact on your health. In the resource section I have included several excellent references and books to help you. Below is a very simple marinade for tofu.

Simple Marinade for Tofu

1	block firm tofu
1 tsp	garlic powder
1 tsp	onion powder
1	bay leaf

| 2 tbsp | Bragg all-purpose seasoning |

Marinate, preferably overnight. Drain and prepare as per recipe.

Tempeh

Tempeh (tem-pay) is a cultured soy product originating from Indonesia. It is considered to be one of the most nutritious soy foods, containing as much as 21 grams of protein in one serving. Tempeh is made from cooked soybeans which are inoculated with a spore and then fermented until the beans bind together in a cottony white filament which is called mycelium. Fermenting makes the tempeh more digestible and also gives it a unique rich and nutty flavour. It can contain only soy or be combined with grains like brown rice, barley, millet, flax or quinoa. It is usually sold frozen in health food stores in 8 or 10 ounce packages. Once the tempeh has defrosted, it will keep in the refrigerator for about 5 days.

Tempeh, in addition to being high in protein, is also rich in vitamin B12, calcium and fiber. It readily absorbs other flavours and is extremely versatile. It can be sliced, cubed, cut into strips, crumbled, fried, braised, grilled, made into burgers; the list is endless.

Tempeh needs to be cooked to be eaten. It can be steamed for 15 minutes or poached in a flavoured broth before using which removes any bitterness and also makes it juicier and easier to absorb flavours.

Basic Steaming Method

If tempeh is frozen simply toss it whole into a steamer and steam for 15 minutes until tender. Alternatively cut tempeh into your desired shape and steam over boiling water for 15 minutes.

Steamed Seasoned Tempeh

1 pkg	tempeh
½ cup	water
2 tbsp	lite tamari

THE BASIC PROTEINS & BUILDING BLOCKS

1 tsp	garlic powder
1 tsp	onion powder
2	bay leaves

Note: Add any flavour you would like to the broth depending on the final outcome of the recipe. Basil, oregano, tarragon, chilies, peppers etc.

Cut tempeh into the shape you will be using later and lay flat in a frying pan. Mix ingredients together and pour over tempeh. Simmer for 10 to 15 minutes turning once. Cool and proceed with recipe.

Tempeh Marinade

1 pkg	tempeh
1 cup	water
½ tbsp	garlic powder
½ tbsp	onion powder
1 tsp	sea salt
2 tbsp	soy sauce or tamari

Marinate tempeh in a bowl with the liquid ingredients and refrigerate for a minimum of 2 hours or overnight. Remove from the broth and continue with the recipe.

For more marinades and sauces, refer to my first book *Dao of Harmony Dawn Cooking: Innovative & Acclaimed Spa Cuisine.*

Seitan

Seitan (pronounced Say-tawn) is a Japanese term meaning "gluten cooked in a soy sauce broth". High in protein and containing very little fat, it absorbs seasonings very well and can be used in many dishes. Cut into strips for stir fries, slice into steaks or burgers, cube for kabobs, grind up and use in spaghetti sauces, or toss into a salad.

It is considered a sustainable food in our house, meaning, it requires little processing, has a long shelf life and can be used in many different ethnic cuisines. I do not consider Seitan a meat substitute. On the contrary, it stands on its own as a tasty high protein food source that can be created effortlessly without harm to the environment. You can purchase seitan ready made at the health food store, but it is much more costly than making it yourself. A 100 calorie serving of seitan provides 15 grams of protein. A 100 calorie serving of hamburger meat yields 5 grams protein, tofu yields 10 grams, and eggs provide 8 grams.

Cooked gluten has been a traditional food staple amongst Chinese and Japanese Buddhists for hundreds of years, providing protein without eating animal flesh. Often called "wheat meat", it has been popular with vegetarians for many years because of its meat-like texture and high nutrient content. It can often be found in Chinese and Japanese restaurants as part of their regular menu.

Traditionally it was made by rinsing the starch and bran from the flour, leaving only the raw wheat gluten. This process although still favored in many parts of the world, is labour and time intensive. Today, instant gluten flour (the starch and bran have been removed) available in health food stores, allows you to make a large batch of protein rich wheat gluten in a fraction of the time. Cooked gluten or seitan keeps for several days in the refrigerator and many months in the freezer.

The method is simple. Liquid is added to instant gluten flour, reconstituting it into a stiff dough which is kneaded briefly and then simmered in a broth after which the cooked gluten/seitan can be used in whatever recipe you like. Depending on the ethnicity of the recipe you are working with, you can add different dry seasonings to the gluten base - chili powder, oregano, thyme, basil, turmeric, chilies and nutritional yeast. Just experiment.

Basic Gluten Recipe
Makes about 3 cups of seitan
1 cup   instant gluten flour

THE BASIC PROTEINS & BUILDING BLOCKS

½ tsp	onion powder
¾ tsp	garlic powder
¾ cup	vegetable stock (pg. 166) or water
2 tbsp	tamari or bragg liquid aminos

Optional ingredients: chopped onion, pepper, chives, tomato paste

Broth

6 cups	vegetable stock (pg. 166)
6 inch piece	kombu, seaweed
5 or 6	dried shiitake mushrooms
3 inch piece	fresh ginger, sliced
½ cup	tamari

Whisk the dry ingredients together in a bowl. In another bowl combine the liquid ingredients and any optional ingredients you would like. Combine the wet and dry ingredients and using a wooden spoon, stir really quickly until both are combined. Remove from bowl and knead on a flat surface until you have a nice smooth ball. Divide into 16 or 20 balls, stretch and press them into cutlets.

In a large pot over medium high heat, combine all broth ingredients together and bring to a boil. Add the wheat cutlets and simmer over very low about 45 minutes.

How to know the seitan is done? Undercooked seitan is hard and rubbery. When it is fully cooked, it is juicy and succulent and ready for use in your recipe. Let cutlets cool in the water and then store in the refrigerator for up to a week in its cooking broth, or drain, wrap appropriately and freeze. Don't throw the broth out as it makes a perfect base for a soup.

Legumes

Legumes are high protein, low-fat food that comes in all shapes, colours and sizes - beans, peas, lentils, peanuts and more. Loaded with vitamins, minerals and dietary fiber, they help combat heart disease, high blood pressure and high cholesterol. They are a good source of complex carbohydrates and they are incredibly inexpensive if purchased dried. They have a long shelf life if stored properly and used in combination with a whole grain such as rice, quinoa or millet, they become a whole protein which is important in the vegetarian diet. Legumes can be sprouted into living foods, which further increase their nutrient and enzyme value. They can then be thrown into soups, salads, sandwiches, mashed on pizza's etc.

Canned beans are very convenient to have on hand, particularly if making a dip or throwing together a salad, but they are expensive and contain high levels of sodium. Canned beans are not sustainable in the sense that they produce a lot of environmental waste due to their manufacturing and packaging. The interior lining of tin cans also contains Bisphenol A (BPA), a toxic chemical used to manufacture polycarbonate plastic and epoxy resins. It is best to use cans sparingly and look for organic beans packed without salt and cans that specify non BPA lining.

Some people have trouble digesting the complex sugars in beans which leads to gas and bloating. In many cases, those who have been used to eating animal products may lack the intestinal flora which is necessary to digest them. It helps to make sure the dried beans have been prepared and cooked properly. They need to be soaked, preferably overnight, which reduces their cooking time and also helps to break down the sugars which cause indigestion. If you use a pressure cooker, it isn't necessary to soak the beans ahead of time. Pressure cooking also cuts back on resources such as water, fuel and your valuable time.

When purchasing beans, make sure they have a nice even coat, not cracked, wrinkly, or chipped, which means they are old. Prior to soaking, check them for stones which is very common considering they are grown from the earth and then rinse them well to remove any dirt. Stones are easier to see amongst the bigger beans but get lost in lentils, particularly red lentils. It is important to note that you should not add anything acidic (vinegar, lemon, wine, tomatoes) to the cooking water of legumes, lentils and peas because it inhibits the cooking process and toughens the bean.

Preparation of Legumes
There are two ways of to prepare the beans, slow or quick.

For slow, soak them for 6-8 hours or overnight in a big pot of cold water covering by about 3 inches. If the weather is hot outside it is better to keep them in the refrigerator as they can ferment. Discard the water, rinse the beans well, cover again with fresh water, bring to a boil for about 10 minutes and then simmer for upwards of an hour and a half, depending on the size of the bean. It is helpful to add a piece of Kombu (seaweed) or spices, which adds vitamins and minerals to the beans and also helps with digestion. Never add salt when cooking beans as it toughens the skins and can make them harder to digest. Beans are done when they are soft and creamy on the inside.

For quick, combine dried beans and water in a pot, bring to a boil and simmer for 2 minutes. Discard water, rinse beans, cover again with fresh water, bring to a boil and simmer as per slow method.

Alternatively, use a pressure cooker which will cook dried beans in next to no time. Follow the manufacturer's instructions on bean cooking and also add a tablespoon of vegetable oil to the pot to prevent excessive foaming which can clog the pressure cooker vent.

Lentils & Peas
Lentils and peas are perfect for everyday meals because they require no soaking and they cook relatively quickly. They are versatile and are used in many different ethnic cuisines. They can be added to soups, stews, dips and pates. They are not only versatile but highly nutritious, containing high levels of protein, iron, fiber and potassium. Lentils are like little seeds and come in all manner of colours - red, green, brown, yellow, white and black, Le Puy.

Peas are small and round and can be green or yellow. They have a higher starch content which makes them creamy and soft when cooked. Larger peas, such as black eyed or chickpeas take longer to cook and are often referred to as beans.

Preparation of Lentils and Peas

Check the lentils and peas thoroughly for dirt and stones and wash in several rinses of water. To cook the lentils, simmer using a ratio of 1 part lentils to 3 parts water or stock, depending on your recipe. The cooking time varies depending on the size of the lentil, anywhere from 10-20 minutes. To cook peas, simmer using a ratio of 1 part pea to 4 parts water or stock for up to an hour. See Split Pea Soup recipe (pg. 168).

Legume Cooking Chart

Beans 1 cup dry	Water (cups)	Cooking time (hours)	Yield (approx)
Adzuki	2 ½	1 ½	2
Anasazi	3	1 – 1 ½	2
Black Beans	3	1 ½ -2	2
Black Eyed Peas	3	1 ½	2
Cannellini	3	1-1 ½	2
Cranberry	3	1-1 ½	2
Garbanzo (chickpeas)	4	1 ½ -2	2
Great Northern	3	1- 1 ½	2
Kidney Beans	3	1 ½ -2	2
*Lentils red	1 ½	15- 25 minutes	2 ¼
*Lentils brown/green	2	30-40 minutes	2 ¼
*Lentils, French	1 ¾	35-45 minutes	2 ¼
Navy Beans	2	1 ½-2	2
Pinto Beans	3	2 -2 ½	2
Soybeans	3	3-4	2
*Split peas green/yellow	4	1	2 ¼

Please note times will change significantly if using a pressure cooker.

The Basic Proteins & Building Blocks

Follow manufacturer's directions. * Note that lentils and split peas do not require pre-soaking.

Grains

Whole grains have historically provided the foundation of the human diet for millennia. Harmony Dawn uses only unrefined grains in our cooking because they contain B vitamins, iron, calcium, phosphorous, potassium, magnesium and zinc. Refined grains are processed thereby stripping them of many essential nutrients and vitamins. There are so many different grains now available due to our global market place that you really can pick and choose which one will suit your menu or your palate. Buy them in bulk because they store well for several months if placed in a glass jar in a cool dark place. They can go rancid if exposed to heat and humidity, so during the summer months it is best to store them in the refrigerator.

Preparation of Grains

The best way to prepare them is to first rinse them well, (with the exception of oats, wheat flakes, spelt flakes, rye flakes). Millet and quinoa can be toasted in a little oil which gives them a nutty flavour. In a saucepan large enough to suit your needs, bring water to a boil, add your grain, return to a boil and simmer until the grain is tender and the water is absorbed. Stirring during cooking is not required. Bulgur and couscous are cooked differently by adding boiling water to them and letting them stand until the water is absorbed.

Rice

There are many different types of rice to choose from to fulfill your dietary needs and requirements. Rice is rich in complex carbohydrates with relatively no fat per serving and it is packed with fiber and B vitamins. Paired with legumes, it becomes a complete protein. Rice is highly versatile and can be served in many formats, from breakfast to dinner to snack food. Most of the world tends to eat white rice which has been processed and stripped of its husk, bran and germ in order to make a polished grain. This refining process also removes the majority of the vitamins and nutrients. The only advantage to eating polished grains and rice is it tends to be a little easier for some people to digest and is faster to prepare. Seniors and people who have trouble chewing also tend to prefer these over whole rice and grains.

Preparation of Rice
Always rinse rice well to remove any dust, dirt or grit that comes from packaging and transportation. Place rice in a saucepan large enough to suit your needs and fill with enough water to cover by about an inch and a half. Bring to a boil, add salt to the water, cover, reduce heat and simmer until the rice has absorbed all of the water. If cooking basmati rice, add 1 tablespoon of butter to the cooking water. White rice will take about 15 minutes but brown will have to cook for at least 40 minutes. For cooking rice, my electric rice cooker is indispensable, since it frees up my stove. Simply plug it in and 45 minutes later, it dings when the rice is done.

Grain and Rice Cooking Chart

Grain 1 cup dry	Water (cups)	Cooking Time	Yield (approx)
Amaranth	3	20-25 minutes	2 ½
Barley, pearl	3	40-50 minutes	3 ½
Basmati , brown	2 ½	35-45 minutes	3
Basmati, white	2	12-20 minutes	3 ¼
Buckwheat groats (kasha)	2	15-20 minutes	2 ½
Bulgur	2	15 minutes	2 ½
Coarse Cornmeal	4	25 minutes	3
Short grain, brown	2 ¼	40-45 minutes	3 ¼
Long grain, brown	2 ½	35-45 minutes	3
Long grain, white	2	15-20 minutes	3 ¼
Millet	2 ½	35-40 minutes	3 ½
Oats	2-2 ½	15-25 minutes	3
Quinoa	2	15-20 minutes	3
*Wild rice	4	35-50 minutes	3

The Basic Proteins & Building Blocks

*Wild rice is not a true rice but the seed of a wild aquatic grass. It was a staple for the Native Indians around the Great Lakes and Rice Lake, where Harmony Dawn is located. It is higher in protein and B vitamins than regular rice.

Rice and Noodle Bowls

Rice bowls usually consist of a bowl of rice topped with a protein like tofu, tempeh or wheat gluten, followed by vegetables and usually a sauce. The rice can be brown, white, jasmine, basmati, black or red... basically any rice that appeals to you. Although popularized right now by main stream vegetarian restaurants, this formula is a centuries old method of preparing and eating food in Asia. It is a complete balance meal.

China, Japan, the Philippines, Singapore, Thailand, India etc., all have different ways of preparing them. Many are unique to the areas from which they have come. They are a balanced and nutritious way of eating food and also fairly inexpensive.

Noodles can be served dry, like in Pad Thai, or in a soup with a flavoured broth like Udon Noodles (pg. 179) which are very popular in Japanese and Vietnamese cooking. Everything you need comes in one bowl, protein, carbohydrates, minerals, nutrients, fiber; it's all there.

Rice and noodles bowls may be served for breakfast, lunch and dinner. In many Asian countries, vegetables are regarded as an important part of the menu, especially highly nutritious leafy green vegetables, healing mushrooms and root vegetables of all kinds.

North American cuisine by contrast is very different. Lunch is usually thought of as a sandwich which is easy to pack in the morning or soup or salad, perhaps a burger and fries or a hotdog. The emphasis is usually on the protein with vegetables and grains being secondary, or non-existent.

Sustainable Fish Sources

Sustainable fish may be defined as seafood from sources either fished or farmed that can exist over the long term without compromising the species survival or the health of the surrounding ecosystem. It is conservation of the resource.*

Between 1950 and 1994, fisherman increased their catch 400% by doubling the number of boats and using more effective fishing methods. The sad fact is that millions of fish - many tons - are thrown away each year as "by catch" due to these practices. It is wanton and wasteful slaughter. Fish are smaller in size and fewer in number; many species are becoming extinct at a rapid rate. Apart from the actual over fishing, the oceans are poisoned and polluted (including sound pollution) and ocean eco systems are breaking down under stress. Jacques Cousteau once pointed out that while we would never dream of eating out of a toilet, we treat our oceans as toilets.

There are things we can do. The choices we make today can and will determine the health of the oceans. Educate yourself. There are many websites dedicated to saving the oceans, Canada Sea Choice www. seachoice.org, Living Oceans Society www.livingoceans.org and *Monterey Bay Aquarium www.monteraybayaquarium.org to name just a few. They keep up-dated lists on the sustainability of all fish from good to bad, which you can conveniently print out and carry with you.

Vote with your wallet. Tell the fish monger at the market what you would like to see and not see. Encourage the restaurants that you frequent to serve ocean friendly fish. Take a stand and in doing so, you can help our oceans.
Eating sustainable fish need not be an expensive proposition. Sardines, anchovies and mackerel are prolific and widespread in the world's oceans. They are growing more plentiful because their predators (tuna, grouper, cod, shark and swordfish) have been over fished, some to the point of extinction. They travel by the billions in enormous schools and feed on plankton. They consume such vast quantities of phytoplankton (algae) that some scientists think sardines might have a positive effect

on climate change. Without them plankton would decompose and produce huge clouds of green house gases contributing to global warming.

Sardines as well as anchovies are considered one of the ocean's very best resources of omega-3 fatty acids, which fight cholesterol, heart disease and high blood pressure. They are rich in protein, iron, phosphorous, potassium and calcium (bones). Aside from being delicious, sardines and anchovies are low in mercury unlike their enormous predators.

Mostly we find these delectable little fish in small tins in the supermarket, but try purchasing them fresh from a reputable fish monger and grilling with a touch of olive oil and lemon. They are loaded with flavour.

*Enjoy a variety of soft melt-in-your mouth Sweet Potato,
Honey and Cumin Buns page 74 and Foccacia Buns page 80 ...*

BAKED GOODS
CHAPTER 1

BAKED GOODS

The aroma of home baked goods is irresistible. Foccacia bread, fresh baked scones and muffins are unfailing crowd pleasers, yet simple to prepare. Television ads would make you think that baking muffins takes all day and is exhausting, which is ridiculous.

Having said that, baking does tend to be more of an exact science than whipping up a stir fry. I have learned that sometimes things are beyond one's control, which is part of being a Baker. Humidity can affect the outcome of your bread and different flours have different needs. Don't let this deter you. Learning new skills takes a little practice and the occasional failure.

Here are some basic quick tips to guide you.

Baking:
- Make sure eggs and butter are at room temperature. Cold batters heat unevenly.
- Stir dry ingredients together and in a separate bowl mix wet ingredients and then combine them together.
- Sift all dry ingredients together. This aerates the flour making a smoother cake.
- If substituting salted butter for unsalted butter do not add extra salt.
- Use separate wooden spoons for sweet mixtures and for savoury.
- Always use non-aluminum baking powder which is found in health food stores.
- When using spelt flour, decrease up to 25% of the liquid that the recipe stipulates.
- Do not over mix muffin or quick bread batter, since this will over stimulate the gluten, leading to a hard end product.
- Always pre-heat the oven.
- Avoid opening the oven while baking to ensure an even temperature. Use your oven light instead to check for doneness.
- Let muffins and quick breads sit in the pan for 5 minutes after baking and then remove promptly to avoid them becoming soggy.
- Temperature for cakes is usually 350° F. Muffins and quick breads

like 375-425° F and pizza likes a really hot 425° F oven.
- When making pastry, the less time you handle it the better. Don't overwork or it won't be flaky.

Bread:
- Breads use active dry yeast to leaven them, whereas cakes, muffins and quick breads use baking powder and baking soda.
- Yeast activates in warm water with a touch of sweetener. The water should be about 110° F or warm to your finger.
- For more detailed information on bread making, please see my first book, *Dao of Harmony Dawn Cooking*.

Frank Smith and Jen Comeau at a cooking workshop

STRAWBERRY WALNUT MUFFINS

Makes 12   VEGAN

When strawberry season hits the farms in our area in early summer, everything becomes strawberry in my kitchen. The aroma and taste of a field strawberry is without compare.

1 cup	fresh strawberries, chopped
2 ripe	bananas, mashed
⅝ cup	almond milk
⅝ cup	maple syrup or agave nectar
1 tsp	vanilla extract
⅔ cup	all-purpose flour
⅔ cup	whole wheat flour
1 tsp	baking powder
½ tsp	baking soda
1 tsp	sea salt
1 tsp	mace
1 cup	walnuts, toasted and chopped

Pre-heat oven to 425⁰ F and have ready 12 paper muffin cups and a muffin pan. In a small bowl combine the bananas, almond milk, maple syrup or agave and vanilla extract. Stir to combine thoroughly.
In a large bowl sift together the flours, baking powder and baking soda. Add the salt, mace and walnuts.

Add the wet ingredients to the dry and stir to just combined, do not overmix or batter will be tough. Spoon the batter into the muffin cups and place in a muffin pan. Bake for 20 minutes or until golden brown. Remove muffins from the pan to cool.

Banana Bran Pecan Muffins

Makes 12

These muffins have a dense hearty flavour. For a vegan alternative omit the eggs and substitute 2 tsp of flax meal whisked into a half cup of water.

2	ripe bananas, mashed
2	eggs, whisked
¾ cup	maple syrup
2 tsp	vanilla extract
½ cup	canola oil
1½ cups	whole wheat flour
1¼ cups	bran
½ tsp	sea salt
1 tbsp	baking powder
1 tsp	nutmeg
½ cup	raisins
½ cup	pecans, toasted & chopped

Pre-heat oven to 400° F and have ready 12 paper muffin cups and a muffin pan. In a small bowl mix together the wet ingredients. In a separate bowl combine dry ingredients. Add the wet to the dry and stir until just combined. Spoon the batter into the muffin cups and place in a muffin pan. Bake for 20 minutes or until golden brown. Remove muffins from the pan to cool.

SWEET PUMPKIN SCONES

Makes about 20

When pumpkins are in season and you can't bear to make another pie, these are perfect. Remove seeds from a small pie pumpkin and roast in the oven for about 45 minutes until tender.

1 cup	whole wheat flour
1½ cups +	all-purpose flour
1 tbsp	baking powder
1 tsp	sea salt
1 tsp	cinnamon
¼ tsp	nutmeg
⅓ cup	organic sugar
⅝ cup	cold unsalted butter (10 tbsp), cut into pieces
1 cup	pumpkin purée
2 tbsp	buttermilk, plus 1 tbsp
2	eggs, lightly whisked

Pre-heat oven to 425° F and line a baking sheet with parchment paper. In a large bowl sift together dry ingredients. Cut in the butter using a knife or your fingers until it resembles coarse meal. In a separate bowl mix together the wet ingredients.

Add the wet ingredients to the dry and stir until until dough holds together. Turn onto a floured surface and lightly knead adding flour as necessary. Shape into 2 balls and roll each ball with a rolling pin into a nice smooth round about 1 inch high. Cut into pie shaped wedges, place on baking sheet, prick with a fork and brush with remaining buttermilk. Bake 10 minutes until golden.

TOMATO PARMESAN SCONES

Makes about 24

These scones are yummy served with scrambled eggs, soup or with a piece of aged cheddar cheese. Serve warm.

1 cup +	whole wheat flour
1 cup	all-purpose flour
1 tbsp	baking powder
¾ tsp	sea salt
1 tsp	fresh ground pepper
1 cup	parmesan cheese, grated
½ cup	cold unsalted butter, cut into pieces
¼ cup	scallions, minced
2 tbsp each	oil packed sun dried tomatoes & green pepper, minced
½ cup +	buttermilk
2	eggs, lightly whisked

Pre-heat oven to 425° F and line a baking sheet with parchment paper. In a large bowl combine flours, salt, pepper, baking power and cheese. Cut in the butter using a knife or your fingers until it resembles coarse meal. In a separate bowl mix together the remaining ingredients.

Make a well in the centre of the dry ingredients and stir in the wet ingredients until you have a sticky dough. Turn dough onto a lightly floured surface and knead, adding more flour as necessary. Roll into a ½ inch patty and cut into circles with a cookie cutter or into pie shapes. Place on baking sheet, prick with a fork and brush with remaining buttermilk. Bake for 10 minutes until golden brown.

SWEET POTATO HONEY & CUMIN BUNS

Makes 12 buns

Using potatoes or sweet potatoes in bread dough creates a lovely light soft bread.

1 medium	sweet potato, about 2 cups, peeled & cubed
2 tsp	honey
1 cup	warm milk about 110° F
1½ tsp	regular active dry yeast
1 cup	whole wheat bread flour
1 cup	unbleached white bread flour
pinch	sweet paprika
1 tsp	cumin
1 tsp	curry powder
1 tsp	sea salt
2 tbsp	melted butter
1 tsp	honey
	cumin seeds for garnish

Steam the sweet potato until tender, let cool slightly and then mash until smooth. In a separate bowl combine the honey, yeast and warm milk and let stand for 10 minutes until foamy. This means the yeast is alive.

Meanwhile combine dry ingredients in a large bowl. Add the milk mixture & sweet potatoes to the dry ingredients and stir, mixing thoroughly until you have a nice smooth dough. Turn onto a lightly floured board and knead about 5 minutes. Place dough in a lightly buttered bowl covered with a damp cloth and allow to rise in a warm draft free place until doubled in size, about an hour.

Punch down and let dough rest for 5 minutes. Divide into 12 pieces and shape into buns. Place on a lightly oiled baking sheet, cover again and let rise another 30 minutes.

Pre-heat oven to 425° F. Combine butter and honey together and drizzle over buns. Sprinkle with the cumin seeds and bake for about 10 minutes until golden brown and fragrant. To check for doneness lightly tap the bottom of a bun with a wooden spoon, if it sounds hollow then the buns are done.

Andy's Meditation Group

Ancho Chili Seed Bread

Makes one large loaf or 12 small buns

This bread combines easy to digest spelt flour, protein packed millet and pumpkin seeds and added calcium from the milk powder.

2 tsp	regular active dry yeast
2 tsp	honey
1½ cups	warm water about 110° F
1 tsp	sea salt
2 tbsp	olive oil
2 tsp	cumin seeds
3 tsp	ancho chili powder
⅓ cup	milk powder, available at grocery stores
¼ cup	millet
¼ cup	pumpkin seeds
½ tsp	fresh ground pepper
2½ cups	spelt flour
½ cup	whole bean flour * see glossary
2 tbsp	guar gum or xanthan gum * see glossary
2 tbsp	melted butter

Have ready a lightly oiled 9 x 5 inch loaf pan for bread or baking sheet for buns. In a small bowl combine the yeast, honey and water and let stand for 10 minutes until foamy. Stir in the salt and oil.

In a large bowl stir together the remainder of the ingredients except the melted butter. Add the yeast mixture and stir with a wooden spoon. When dough is firm enough to handle turn onto a lightly floured board and knead for 5 minutes adding additional spelt flour as needed. This is a sticky moist dough so be careful not to add too much flour which can make the dough too heavy.

Transfer the dough to a lightly oiled bowl and cover with a damp cloth. Allow to rise in a warm draft free place until doubled in size, about 1½ hours. Punch the dough down and let rest for 5 minutes. Turn onto your counter and shape into a loaf the size of your bread pan with ends of loaf touching the ends of the pan. Alternatively roll into a log and cut into equal 2 inch pieces, shape into round buns and place on a lightly oiled baking sheet. Use a sharp knife to score the top of the loaf with 3 diagonal slashes about ¼ inch deep, for the buns, slash once. Cover again and let rise another 30 minutes or until doubled.

Pre-heat oven to 375º F. Brush with the melted butter and bake for 35 minutes or until fragrant and golden. To test for readiness, pull bread from pan and tap the bottom with a wooden spoon. If it sounds hollow the bread is done.

WHOLE WHEAT HERB BAGUETTE

Makes about 2 large loaves

This classic bread is crusty on the outside and soft on the inside. Serve on its own or as a base for Mediterranean Bean Crostini (pg. 234). If using dried herbs substitute 1 tsp for each tbsp of fresh herbs.

2½ cups	warm water, about 110° F
1 tbsp	honey
2 tbsp	fast acting yeast
5½ cups or so	whole wheat bread flour
1 tbsp	sea salt
1 tsp	fresh ground pepper
1-2 tbsp	fresh herbs of choice; rosemary, thyme or dill plus extra for garnish
1	egg white, whisked with 1 tbsp water
	coarse sea salt

In a large bowl stir together 1 cup of flour with the water, honey and yeast. Set aside covered with a towel for about 15 to 20 minutes until puffy. Stir down with a wooden spoon and add salt, pepper, herbs and remaining flour 1 cup at a time. When you can no longer stir flour in, turn dough onto a floured board and knead, adding remaining flour ½ cup at a time until you have a nice soft dough ball.

Transfer to a lightly oiled bowl covered with a damp towel and let rise in a warm draft free place for about an hour, or until doubled in size.

Pre-heat oven to 450° F. Punch down the dough and turn onto a lightly floured surface and knead for a minute or two. Cut into 2 loaves and roll each loaf into a nice long baguette. Sprinkle a cookie sheet with cornmeal and transfer baguettes to sheet. Cover and let rise another

15 minutes. Make 4 or 5 diagonal slashes on the loaves and brush with the egg white mixture. Sprinkle with coarse salt and and extra herbs.

Bake for about 30 minutes until golden brown. To make an extra crispy crust, mist the loaves every 10 minutes with water.

FOCCACIA BUNS WITH ROSEMARY & PINE NUTS

Makes about 15 buns   VEGAN

Foccacia bread is soft, fragrant and savoury. Make small buns and serve with soup or larger buns that you can stuff with grilled vegetables.

Dough

2 tsp	regular active dry yeast
1 cup	warm water about 110° F
2 tbsp	honey or agave nectar
2 tbsp	olive oil
1 tsp	sea salt
½ cup	pine nuts reserving 2 tsp
2 tbsp	fresh rosemary, chopped
3 cups	whole wheat bread flour

Topping

4	garlic cloves, minced
2 tbsp	olive oil
1 tbsp	fresh rosemary, chopped
½	red onion cut into thin slivers
	coarse sea salt & fresh ground pepper

In a large bowl combine the warm water with the honey and yeast and let stand about 10 minutes until foamy. Stir in the oil, salt, pine nuts rosemary and 1 cup of flour. Add the remaining flour a ½ cup at a time until the dough begins to stick together. It should feel soft but also a little sticky. Add more flour if dough is wet.

Turn the dough onto a floured work surface and knead for about 5 minutes adding more flour if necessary. Transfer the dough to a lightly oiled bowl and cover with a damp cloth. Allow to rise in a warm draft free place until doubled in size, about 1½ hours.

Punch the dough down and let rest for 5 minutes. Turn onto a lightly floured surface and roll into a log. Cut into equal sized pieces about an inch thick. Shape into round buns and place on a lightly oiled baking sheet. Cover again and let rise another 30 minutes until doubled in size. Pre-heat oven to 350° F.

In a small bowl mix together the garlic and the olive oil. Make small indentations in the dough with your fingers and smear the olive oil mixture all over the dough. Sprinkle with the rosemary, sea salt, pepper, pine nuts and onion. Bake for about 30 minutes until puffed and golden. Let cool about 10 minutes and serve.

PISSALADIERE

Makes two, 10 x 15 inch pans   VEGAN

This is a thin soft flatbread topped with sweet caramelized onions. It is usually served with salty anchovies so feel free to add those along with any of the other variations below.

Dough

1 tbsp	regular active dry yeast
1 cup	warm water about 110° F
1 tbsp	honey or agave nectar
3 tbsp	olive oil
1 tsp	sea salt
¼ cup	cornmeal
2 cups	whole wheat bread flour or spelt flour

Topping

3 tbsp	olive oil
3-5 cups	onions, thinly sliced
2 tsp	fresh thyme
1 tsp	fresh ground pepper
1 cup	kalamata olives, chopped
Variations:	grated parmesan cheese, anchovy filets, roasted peppers, green olives, assorted herbs

In a large bowl combine the warm water with the honey and yeast and let stand about 10 minutes until foamy. Stir in the oil, salt, cornmeal and 1 cup of flour. Add the remaining flour a ½ cup at a time until the dough begins to stick together. Turn onto a lightly floured surface and knead for about 5 minutes adding more flour as necessary. The dough will be slightly sticky. Form into a ball and transfer to a lightly oiled bowl and cover with a damp cloth. Allow to rise in a warm draft free place until doubled in size, about 1 hour.

Meanwhile in a large pot over medium low heat cook the onions in the oil until they turn golden brown and are sticky and soft. This could take up to 45 minutes. Add the thyme and pepper and remove from heat.

Pre-heat oven to 400° F and lightly oil 2 baking sheets. Punch the dough down to release the air and turn onto a floured surface. Divide the dough in half and roll each out to a very thin rectangle. Sprinkle cornmeal lightly onto baking sheets and tranfer dough to sheets. Smear the onions, olives and a twist of black pepper and bake for 20 minutes or until edges turn golden brown.

WHOLE WHEAT PASTRY

Makes enough for two, 9 inch pies

This recipe comes from my mom Margaret who is a real master of pastry making. Try not to overwork the pastry and make sure you let it rest for about 30 minutes. Butter is what makes pastry flaky but you can substitute safflower or canola oil for a vegan alternative and still obtain excellent results.

2½ cups	whole wheat flour
1 tsp	organic sugar
1 tsp	sea salt
1¼ cups	unsalted butter, chilled, cut into chunks alternatively use 1 cup oil

I use my food processor because it is fast and I don't handle the dough much which is key to a flaky pastry. If you use a bowl and spoon work fast.

Pulse together the flour, sugar, salt and butter in a food processor until fine. Trickle ⅓ cup of chilled water until mixture binds together. If you add too much liquid the dough will clump together and it will be too wet. If using oil instead of butter be careful of this. Remove dough from processor and shape into two rounds. Wrap each round in wax paper and refrigerate for 30 minutes. Remove and let rest for 10 minutes and then roll out pastry on a lightly floured board.

A half full dishwasher uses the same amount of water and power as a full dishwasher

Choux Puff Pastry

Makes about 15 pastry shells

This is one of the easiest pastries to make. It is light and crispy and can be used to make éclairs, profiteroles or savoury appetizers. Steam is created during baking which expands the pastry giving it volume. The outside is golden and crispy and the inside fairly hollow, which makes them perfect for stuffing. For sweet éclairs, fill the pastry with Chocolate Icing (pg. 259) and top with Cocoa Demi-Glaze (pg. 257), or Strawberry Almond Cream (pg. 283).

1 cup	all-purpose flour
⅛ tsp	sea salt
1 cup	water or milk
⅓ cup	unsalted butter
4	eggs, room temperature

Pre-heat oven to 400° F and lightly oil a baking sheet. Combine flour and salt in a bowl. In a pot over medium heat add the liquid and butter and bring to a low boil. Add the flour all at once and stir quickly with a wooden spoon until you have a smooth paste that pulls away from the sides of the pot. Remove from heat. Add eggs one at a time beating vigorously after each egg. The dough will be glossy and firm.

Spoon tablespoons of dough onto the baking sheet, alternatively use a piping bag to create long éclair shapes. Sprinkle with a touch of water and bake for 10 minutes. Reduce heat to 350° F and bake another 25 minutes until golden. Turn off oven and let sit in oven until the shell is hardened. Remove from oven and let cool. Slice in half and remove any wet dough inside prior to filling. Store in a container and prior to serving fill with your choice of filling.

Whole Wheat Pizza Dough

Makes two, 15 inch pizza's VEGAN

Homemade pizza is a real treat and it could not be easier to prepare. Use spelt flour or a combination of different flours to come up with your own personal dough.

1 cup	warm water about 110° F
2 tbsp	honey or agave nectar
1 tsp	regular active dry yeast
2 tbsp	olive oil
1 tsp	sea salt
1½ cups	whole wheat flour
¾ cup	all-purpose flour
2 tbsp	ground flax seeds

In a large bowl combine the warm water with the honey and yeast and let stand about 10 minutes until foamy. Add the oil, salt and whole wheat flour and stir using a wooden spoon. Add the remaining flour and flax seeds stirring until the dough is firm. Transfer to a floured surface and knead for about 5 minutes adding more water to prevent sticking.

Place in a lightly oiled bowl covered with a damp towel and let rise in a warm spot for 1½ hours or until doubled in size. Punch the dough down and let rest for 5 minutes. Sprinkle baking sheets lightly with cornmeal. Divide dough in half and roll out thinly to fit the baking sheet. Proceed with your pizza toppings.

BEAN & FLAX SEED CRACKERS

Makes about 2 dozen

This is a gluten free cracker made with whole bean flour which has been ground from dried white beans. It is available at health stores and the Bulk Barn.

1 cup	whole bean flour
1 tsp	xanthan gum * see glossary
½ tsp	sea salt
¼ tsp	fresh ground pepper
2 tbsp	flax seeds, lightly ground
½ tsp	honey
¼ cup	buttermilk or yogurt
2 tbsp	olive oil

Pre-heat oven to 400° F and lightly oil a baking sheet. In a large bowl combine the flour, gum, salt, pepper and flax seeds. Stir in the milk and oil to form a crumbly dough. Turn onto a a lightly floured surface and knead into a ball.

Divide the dough in half and place each half between sheets on parchment paper. Roll out to a thickness of ⅛ inch. Prick with a fork and cut into small crackers and arrange on the baking sheets. Bake for about 15 minutes until golden. Turn crackers over and bake the other side until golden.

Fix water leaks. A dripping faucet can add up to lost water and lost money

MEDITERRANEAN SUN DRIED TOMATO & OLIVE BREAD

Makes two, 8 x 4 inch loaves

This is a quick bread, meaning it is leavened with baking powder and not active dry yeast. Preparation time is fast and the resulting bread is a soft tasty loaf that is perfect with soup, stew or simply on its own warm, drizzled with olive oil.

1½ cups	all-purpose flour
1½ cups	whole wheat flour
2 tsp	baking powder
1 tsp	sea salt
2 tbsp	brown sugar
1 cup	parmesan cheese, grated
1 tsp	garlic powder
1 tsp	dried rosemary
1 tsp	black pepper
2	free range eggs
1½ cups	buttermilk
3 tbsp	olive oil
½ cup	sun dried tomatoes, chopped
½ cup	kalamata olives, chopped
2 tbsp	capers, minced
½ cup	parsley, chopped

Butter or oil 2 loaf pans and set aside. Pre-heat oven to 375° F. In a small bowl combine all the dry ingredients. In a large bowl whisk together the eggs, buttermilk and oil. Stir in remaining ingredients. Add the flour mixture to the wet ingredients and stir until just combined. Divide equally among the 2 pans and bake for 35 minutes or until tester comes out clean. Remove and let cool.

Whole Wheat & Spelt Tortilla Wraps

8 wraps

Homemade wraps are very easy to make and well worth your effort. They keep for a few days and also freeze well so make a big batch to have on hand. Substitute 2 tablespoons of cooked brown rice for the flax seeds for a hearty alternative.

1 cup	whole wheat
1 cup	spelt flour
½ tsp	baking powder
½ tsp	coarse salt
2 tbsp	flax seeds, ground slightly
5 tbsp	plain yogurt
⅔ cup	buttermilk

In a large bowl stir together dry ingredients. Add buttermilk and yogurt and combine to make a nice smooth dough. Add more flour if the dough is too sticky. Turn onto a lightly floured surface and knead for 5 minutes. Cover with plastic wrap and let rest for 30 minutes.

Cut into 8 equal pieces. Using a rolling pin, roll them out to about ⅛ inch thick. Place on a parchment paper lined baking sheet with parchment between each wrap. Cover with a damp towel and let rest for another 30 minutes.

In a non-stick skillet over medium heat, cook each tortilla wrap until golden brown spots appear and they are puffy, about a minute per side. Transfer to a plate or store in the fridge/freezer separated with parchment paper until needed.

OAT PIE CRUSTS

Each recipe makes one, 9 inch pie crust

Here are 2 alternatives to butter rich pastry crusts.

Maple Oat   *VEGAN*

1½ cups	rolled oats
½ cup	whole wheat pastry flour
¼ cup	water
¼ cup	safflower oil
¼ cup	maple syrup
½ cup	ground nut of choice: walnut, almond, pecan
pinch	sea salt

Pre-heat oven to 350° F. Grind oats in a food processor. Add remaining ingredients and pulse to combine. Press evenly into a lightly oiled pie pan and bake for 10 minutes.

Honey Coconut

2 cups	rolled oats
¼ cup	finely shredded coconut, toasted
1 tsp	vanilla extract
⅓ cup	corn oil
¼ cup	honey

Prepare as per Maple Oat crust.

COCONUT HONEY CHEESECAKE CRUST

Makes one 9 ½ inch crust

3	egg whites
2 ¼ cups	shredded unsweetened coconut, large flakes
¼ cup	honey
¼ cup	all-purpose flour

Pre-heat oven to 350⁰ F and lightly oil a 9 ½ inch spring form pan. Toast coconut in a small pan over medium low heat until golden. In a medium size bowl lightly whisk egg whites until frothy. Whisk in honey and flour until combined. Stir in coconut.

Press coconut mixture into base and up sides of pan by a ½ an inch. Bake for 25 minutes until set and golden.

Sweet Avocado Cocoa Tart with Coconut Honey Cheesecake Crust

A start to the day Harmony Dawn style - Homemade Granola page 97, fluffy Tomato Pesto Omelette page 99 and Strawberry Walnut Muffins page 70...

BRUNCH & LUNCH
CHAPTER 2

Brunch & Lunch

Breakfast and lunch are very important meals, but people generally don't have much time to prepare them. Many nutrition specialists feel that breakfast is the most important meal of the day. Coming off a night time fast, your body needs sufficient fuel to propel you through the busy day ahead. Lunch is that well deserved break in the day when you can refuel and recharge to take you through the rest of the day. Brunch is a celebration meal, a cross between breakfast and lunch. It could be a time spent with friends over the weekend or lounging with your family without a set schedule.

In the following section, I have tried to include breakfast, brunch and lunch meals that are easy to prepare, nutritious and kid friendly. Check out the the Soup, Salads, Vegetables and Sides chapters for other lunch time fare. Use your creativity in your weekly meal and shopping planning. For example, a dinner of Black Bean Burgers (pg. 192) is awesome the next day in a pita with some greens or rolled in a tortilla wrap; the left over rice can be turned into a cereal the next morning.

Here are some extra tips to help you.

- Make a large batch of granola and store in small vacuum sealed bags. It will last a couple of weeks or more.
- Use quick cooking quinoa, couscous or bulgur for a super fast porridge. Serve with fresh berries, warm almond milk, toasted nuts and maple syrup. Time saver - use left over grains and re-heat gently.
- Asparagus Quiche (pg. 100) can be taken to work in a container for lunch. Throw in a side salad and a piece of pita to complete the meal.
- Left over Black Bean & Avocado Quesadilla mixture (pg. 104) can be rolled into a tortilla wrap. Add lettuce, tomatoes and grated cheese.
- Roll leftover grain salads (see salad section) into tortilla wraps or use lettuce or kale as your wrap.
- Using a pita pocket, line with White Bean Basil Dip (pg. 243) and fill with vegetables and roasted tofu or tempeh.
- Roll left over Nasi Goreng into rice balls. They can be stuffed into a pita drizzled with Peanut Sauce (pg. 149). Add shredded lettuce.

- If you don't have a fridge or toaster oven at work, convince your employer to purchase them so you can bring your lunch to work.

Sauteed Vegetable Quesadillas page 104

Pecan Banana Buttermilk Pancakes

Makes 12 large

Serve these hearty pancakes topped with mashed bananas and yogurt and a sprinkle of maple syrup.

2	eggs
2 cups	buttermilk
2 tsp	vanilla extract
2 tbsp	molasses
¾ cup	whole wheat flour
¾ cup	all-purpose flour
2 tbsp	wheat germ
¾ tsp	mace
pinch	sea salt
1½ tsp	baking powder
½ tsp	baking soda
½ cup	toasted pecans, chopped
1	banana, sliced
2 tbsp	unsalted butter
2 tbsp	vegetable oil

Whisk together the first 4 ingredients and set aside. In a separate bowl sift together dry ingredients. Add wet to dry and stir until just combined. Do not overmix as this will result in hard cakes.

In a large frying pan over medium high heat, melt butter and oil. Scoop about ⅓ cup per cake into the pan and top with a few pieces of the banana. Wait until you see bubbles appearing and then flip. Pancakes are done when both sides are a nice golden brown. Keep warm in oven until serving.

MACADAMIA PECAN & CRANBERRY GRANOLA

Makes 11 cups

Macadamia nuts are buttery, meaty and high in fibre with an
exotic flare. Granola usually lasts about 2 weeks properly sealed in
a container. Add the dried fruit as you need to prevent them from
becoming too hard. Flax meal can be found in most supermarkets and
health food stores.

6 cups	organic quick oats
1 cup	macadamia nuts, coarsely chopped
1¼ cups	pecans, chopped
½ cup	ground flax meal
½ cup	wheat germ
½ cup	sunflower seeds
1 tsp	mace
½ tsp	vanilla extract
⅔ cup	safflower oil
⅔ cup	maple syrup
½ cup	dried cranberries
½ cup	Thompson's raisins

Pre-heat oven to 300° F. In a large bowl combine all dry ingredients
except fruit. In a small bowl stir together oil, maple syrup and vanilla
then pour over dry ingredients mixing thoroughly with a wooden
spoon. Spread granola onto a baking sheet and bake for approximately
45 minutes stirring once or twice to ensure even baking.

Remove from the oven when golden brown and return to the bowl.
Allow to cool and store accordingly. Add dried fruit as needed.

Gluten Free Cereal

Makes 5 cups

Buckwheat is not a grain, it is the fruit of a relative of rhubarb, *Fagopyrum esculentum*. It is cultivated in cold climates, tolerates poor soil and matures in a little over 60 days. Buckwheat also contains all essential amino acids. Serve with warm milk or soy milk.

3 cups	buckwheat flakes, available at health food stores
½ cup	sunflower seeds
½ cup	hulled hemp seeds
½ cup	Brazil nuts, chopped
½ cup	walnuts, chopped
¼ cup	flax seeds, lightly ground
1½ tsp	cinnamon
1 tsp	nutmeg
½ cup	flax oil
2 tsp	vanilla extract
6 tbsp	agave nectar
½ cup	dried apricots, chopped
½ cup	chopped dehydrated strawberries, optional

Pre-heat oven to 300° F. Combine flakes, seeds, nuts and spices together in a large bowl. In a separate small bowl stir together the oil, vanilla and agave nectar and then pour over dry ingredients.

Spread the cereal onto a large baking sheet and bake for about 30-45 minutes until golden brown and fragrant, stirring every 15 minutes. Remove from oven and stir in strawberries and apricots. Cool and then store in a container.

Fluffy Tomato Pesto Omelette

Serves 2

Omelettes can be served for breakfast, lunch or dinner. Experiment by adding what ever you have on hand, left over cooked broccoli or cauliflower, sprouts, black beans, fried mushrooms or zucchini, swiss or cheddar cheese, steamed kale or chard…

2 tbsp	unsalted butter
4	eggs, separated
2 tbsp	milk or soy milk
2	scallions, chopped
⅓ cup	tomatoes, chopped
1 tbsp	spinach pesto sauce (pg. 151)
¼ cup	fresh chopped spinach
¼ cup	fresh parmesan cheese, grated
	sea salt & fresh ground pepper

In a small bowl whisk egg yolks until smooth. In a separate bowl beat the egg whites until foamy, add the yolks and milk and stir to combine.

In a 12 inch frying pan melt the butter over medium high heat and sauté the scallions until soft. Pour the egg mixture into the pan and sprinkle with a pinch of salt and pepper. Cover and turn heat to medium low. When omelette has puffed up and is mostly cooked through, spoon the tomatoes, pesto, spinach and grated cheese over one half and cook for another minute or so. Flip the plain side on top of the vegetables. Cut in half and serve.

Asparagus Quiche

Serves 4

Serve for breakfast, lunch or dinner with boiled new potatoes with mint and a light maché green salad.

Pastry for a 9 inch pie (pg. 84)

1 cup	asparagus, cut into ½ inch pieces, blanched
2	asparagus stalks cut in half, blanched
2 tbsp	unsalted butter
½ tsp	sea salt
¼ tsp	fresh ground pepper
1½ cups	onions, chopped
2 cups	gruyère cheese, grated
1 tbsp	all-purpose flour
3	eggs
1 cup	half & half cream
pinch	cayenne pepper

Pre-heat oven to 425° F. Roll out pastry and line pan. To blanch asparagus, place in a small pan of boiling salted water for about 4 minutes. Remove and plunge into ice cold water. Dry and set aside.

In a frying pan over medium high heat sauté the onions, salt and pepper in the butter until soft. Place in the bottom of the prepared pastry pan topped with the ½ inch pieces of asparagus. Toss grated cheese with flour and add to pie. Whisk together the eggs, cream and cayenne and pour over top of the cheese. Decorate with remaining asparagus stalks and bake for 10 minutes. Turn oven down to 325° F and bake for 35-45 minutes until puffy and golden brown and the middle of the pie feels set. Remove from oven and let sit 15 minutes before serving.

EGG FOO YOUNG

Serves 6

This is a dense Asian omelette that you can slice into pieces straight out of the pan. Usually served with rice and stir fried vegetables.

2 tsp	canola oil
3 tsp	sesame oil
⅓ cup	scallions, chopped
1 tbsp	red pepper, minced
2 tsp	soy sauce
1 tsp	mirin
½ tsp	chili oil
pinch	honey
4	eggs, whisked
¼ tsp	dried chilies, optional
¼ cup	mung bean sprouts
1 tbsp	chives, chopped
	cooked baby shrimp, optional
	fresh shiitake mushrooms, chopped & optional

Pre-heat oven to broil. Whisk together the eggs, 1 tsp sesame oil, soy sauce, mirin, chili oil, honey and dried chilies then set aside.

In a large oven proof frying pan over medium heat, sauté the scallions, red pepper and shiitakes (if using) in the canola and remaining sesame oil until tender. Add the egg mixture and cover cooking about 2 minutes to allow bottom to cook. Transfer to the middle shelf of the oven and cook about 5 minutes until set. Remove, sprinkle with the bean sprouts and chives and serve with oyster sauce if desired.

Homemade Mix & Match Pizza's

Pizza's are easy. Your crust can be either a wrap (pg. 89) or the more traditional pizza dough (pg. 86). Mix and match base and toppings from the selections below.

Base Selections:

tomato sauce, spinach pesto, arugula pesto, sun dried tomato pesto, black olive tapenade, mashed white beans, chick peas or black beans, olive oil & garlic, olive oil & fresh herbs, caramelized onions & fresh rosemary, classic hummus, roasted red pepper sauce.

Topping Selections:

cheeses like ceddar, Swiss, feta, grano padano, parmesan, havarti, chevre; artichoke hearts, capers, steamed vegetables, broccoli, cauliflower, fresh leafy greens such as chopped romaine, spinach, arugula, mustard greens, Swiss chard, kale; fresh dill, basil, coriander, thyme or oregano, roasted vegetables such as potatoes, sweet potatoes, beets and parsnips; roasted tofu, tempeh and seitan; smoked Pacific salmon, Albacore tuna, mackerel, sardines, anchovies; olives of any kind such as kalamata, green or black; red onion, fresh avocado, fresh tomatoes, roasted tomatoes and sun dried tomatoes.

If using wrap crust, prepare recipe (pg. 89) and place on baking sheet. Add your base and toppings and bake 400° F for 5 minutes until crispy.

If using pizza dough, prepare recipe (pg. 86). Roll out dough to desired shape and size - one large size or individual small pizzas. Sprinkle cornmeal on the baking sheet, place dough on sheet and add base and toppings. Brush edges with olive oil, place on bottom shelf in oven and bake at 400° F for about 12 to 15 minutes until golden brown.

SMOKED SALMON & POTATO PIZZA

Makes 1 large 15 inch pie

Here is an example of using mix and match ingredients. Enjoy!

Pizza dough for one pizza (pg. 86)

1 small pkg	Pacific smoked salmon, torn into pieces
2 cups	small new potatoes, cooked & sliced
1 small	red onion, sliced thinly
½ cup or so	arugula pesto, (pg. 156)
1 tbsp	capers
1 cup	feta cheese, crumbled
1 cup	fresh arugula leaves
	cornmeal for pan

Pre-heat oven to 400° F and sprinkle cornmeal over a baking sheet. Roll out dough with a rolling pin and place on the baking sheet gently stretching to fill the sheet.

Spread pesto over base, followed by potatoes, salmon, onions, capers, arugula and lastly feta cheese. Bake for about 12 minutes on the bottom shelf or until crust is golden brown.

Recycle all recyclable materials and compost your organic kitchen waste

BLACK BEAN & AVOCADO QUESADILLAS

Serves 4

This recipe has a Mexican accent and goes well with Jade Rice Pilaf (pg. 239). Make your own healthy Tortilla Wrap (pg. 89) or buy good quality whole wheat wraps from the health food store.

8	medium tortillas wraps about 7 inches wide
1½	large ripe avocados, peeled, flesh removed & mashed
1	green onion, minced
1 tbsp	lime juice
¼ cup	red pepper, minced
¼ tsp	fresh ground pepper
¾ tsp	garlic powder
1 tsp	ground cumin
1½ tsp	coarse sea salt
2-3 drops	Tabasco or your favourite hot sauce
1 cup	black beans, cooked
½ cup each	cheddar cheese & Monterey jack cheese, grated
1 tsp	olive oil

I use a grill pan on top of the stove but you can bake them on a baking sheet in a 350° F oven. Place all ingredients except cheese in a bowl and stir well. Divide the mixture equally amongst 4 of the wraps, spreading to within ½ of an inch to the edge.

Sprinkle with the cheese and top with remaining 4 wraps. Over medium high heat brush the grill pan with oil and cook each quesadilla until grill marks appear, about 3-4 minutes. Repeat on other side. Remove and cut into wedges.

SAUTEED VEGETABLE QUESADILLAS

Serves 4

It takes very little time to prepare these quesadillas. Serve with a side of sour cream and tomato salsa along with a tossed green salad.

8	medium tortillas wraps about 7 inches wide
1 tbsp	olive oil
2 small	yellow onions, slivered
2	portabello mushrooms cut into 1 inch pieces
½	red pepper, cut into ½ inch slices
1 small	zucchini, as above
pinch each	sea salt and fresh ground pepper
1 tsp	dried basil
½ tsp	dried oregano
1 cup	mozzarella cheese
1 cup	cheddar cheese

In a small frying pan over medium high heat sauté the onion in the oil until tender. Add the remaining vegetables and sprinkle with the salt, pepper, basil and oregano and continue to cook until mushrooms begin to release their liquid.

Pre-heat oven to 350⁰ F. Divide the mixture equally amongst 4 of the wraps, spreading to within ½ of an inch to the edge. Sprinkle with the cheese and top with remaining 4 wraps. Transfer to a baking sheet and bake for about 6 minutes per side or until crisp and cheese is nice and soft. Remove from oven and cut into wedges.

Quinoa & Avocado Wraps

Serves 2

Serve these nutritious wraps with a big green salad and Lemon Parsley Dressing (pg. 147). Recipe easily doubles to serve more people.

½ cup	cooked quinoa, see glossary on cooking method
½	of a large fresh avocado, about ⅓ cup
1 tsp	lemon juice
½ tsp	nutritional yeast
¼ tsp	garlic powder
½ tsp	Bragg all purpose seasoning
pinch	sea salt & fresh pepper
1	carrot, grated
1	beet, grated
handful	fresh baby spinach
2 - 4	6 inch wraps, homemade if possible (pg. 89)
Variations:	julienne of fresh peppers or cucumber, sprouts, roasted tofu or tempeh

In a small bowl mash avocado with a fork until smooth. Add the lemon juice, spices and quinoa and stir to combine. Taste and adjust seasonings.

Lay your wraps on the counter and divide the mixture in half spreading to within ¾ of an inch of the perimeter. Layer the carrot and beet in the bottom ⅓ of the wrap. Add the spinach and any optional variations and roll from the bottom up pulling in the sides to form a neat pocket. Slice in half and serve.

SPICY CORN QUESADILLAS

Serves 2-4

Quesadillas are super fast to prepare and always seem to be a crowd pleaser. Serve with your favourite tomato salsa and if you don't mind a few extra calories, sour cream.

1	large ripe avocado
1 cup	corn, cooked
1 large	shallot, minced
¼ tsp	garlic powder
¼ tsp	jalapeno, minced or cayenne pepper
¼ tsp	coarse sea salt
¼ tsp	cumin
2 tbsp	prepared medium spicy salsa
6	small wraps 6 inches (pg. 89) or store bought
1 cup or so	cheddar cheese, grated

In a small bowl mash the avocado. Add remaining ingredients except the wraps and cheese. Stir to combine. Taste and adjust if necessary. Divide mixture amongst 3 of the wraps, spreading to within ½ of an inch to the edge. Sprinkle with the cheese making sure you come close to the edges. Place remaining wraps on top.

Bake or use a grill pan on top of the stove. If baking, heat oven to 350º F and place on a baking sheet. Flip after about 7 minutes. If using a grill pan sprinkle with a touch of olive oil and grill over medium heat about 4 minutes per side or until you have nice grill lines and the cheese is melted. Cut into wedges and serve.

LEAFY SALAD WRAPS

Serves 4

Use any large green leaf you like such as romaine, steamed kale, beet or Swiss chard greens. Serve with a side of vegetable crudites and extra pesto. Add Roasted Tempeh (pg. 223) for an extra protein boost.

1-2 heads	Boston Bibb lettuce or any large leaf lettuce
2	large portabella mushrooms, sliced in ½ inch pieces
1-2	zucchini, sliced in ½ & then in ¼ inch long pieces
12	asparagus spears
1	red pepper, roasted & sliced in ½ inch wide pieces
1 cup	mayo or nayo
3 - 4 tbsp	arugula almond pesto (pg.156)
	fresh chives, kept long
	olive oil, coarse sea salt & fresh ground pepper

Pre-heat oven to broil. Place all vegetables on a baking sheet and brush with oil. Sprinkle with salt and pepper. Roast in top third of oven until golden brown, turn and repeat on other side. Roast only until vegetables begin to release their juice. Remove from oven. Soak chives in simmering water for a few seconds to soften. Remove and dry.

In a small bowl mix together the mayo and pesto sauce. Using only the largest of the lettuce leaves place the vegetables evenly in the centre and smear 1-2 tbsp of sauce over them. Roll the lettuce around the vegetables and gently tie with the chives to secure.

Turn off the tap while brushing your teeth or shaving and save about 80% of clean water going down the drain

Apple Baked Beans

Makes 8 hearty servings

I love baked beans any time of the day. The classic is baked beans on toast but they are versatile. For example you can roll them in a wrap topped with tomatoes and cheese. They contain protein, loads of essential dietary fiber and they taste great whether spicy, sweet or savoury. Use dried beans that have been soaked as you will need the cooking water, see (pg. 58) for soaking method.

6 cups	cooked navy beans, about 3 cups dried
1 tbsp	olive oil
2 cups	yellow onions, sliced
1 cup	red onion, sliced
2 tsp	sea salt
2 tsp	grain mustard
1 tbsp	dried hot mustard
¼ cup	apple butter
2 tbsp	molasses
¼ cup	maple syrup
5 tbsp	tomato paste
2 cups	reserved bean cooking liquid

Pre-heat oven to 275° F and lightly oil a large roasting pan. In a large pot over medium heat sauté the onions and salt in the oil until golden brown and caramelized, about 45 minutes. Add the beans and remaining ingredients stirring to combine well.

Transfer to the roasting pan, cover and bake for 3 hours stirring every 30 minutes. Serve or allow to cool and freeze in smaller portions.

Baguettes with Grilled Pesto Vegetables

Serves 4-6

These are always a hit and are relatively simple to make if you use store bought baguettes and pesto sauce. For the more adventurous and creative make your own Whole Wheat Herb Baguette (pg. 78) and Spinach Pesto (pg. 151).

1	whole grain baguette
1-2	zucchini, cut into thirds & then ¼ inch long pieces
4	portabella mushrooms, sliced in ½ inch long pieces
1 large	red pepper, roasted & sliced in ½ inch long pieces
12 large	basil leaves
1 pkg	sliced provolone cheese, optional
1½ cups	mayonnaise
3 tbsp	pesto sauce
	olive oil for brushing, coarse sea salt & fresh pepper
Variations:	sun dried tomatoes, roasted fresh tomatoes, roasted asparagus

To roast red peppers, place on a lightly oiled baking sheet and roast in a 425° F oven for about 20 minutes, turning every 5 minutes. Pepper should be black. Remove from oven and place in a bowl covered with a plate for 10 minutes to cool. When cool enough to handle, remove seeds and slice. Keep oven on.

Place zucchini and mushrooms on a lightly oiled baking sheet. Brush them with oil and sprinkle with the salt and pepper. Roast in the oven for about 5 minutes turning them when golden. Repeat on other side. Remove and set aside.

Slice the baguette in half lengthwise and place in oven to toast lightly, about 1 minute.

In a small bowl mix together the pesto and the mayonnaise and spread on each baguette section. Layer the vegetables on top finishing with a basil leaf topped with the provolone. Place back in the oven and roast until cheese is bubbly and melted.

Margaret Lawrence & Nicola

Savoury Indonesian Gado Gado Salad with warm Peanut Sauce page124 ...

SALADS

Salads have come along way since the basic iceberg lettuce and Ranch dressing days.

Salad greens are available in an array of types and combinations, which can be found in our local supermarkets. Venture into a farmers market and you will find even more unusual types that are grown in smaller batches.

Salads are an opportunity to create healthy enzyme and nutrient rich dishes that are a welcome addition to a meal or served as the centerpiece.

Salads can be hot or cold; they can be made with a base of greens, grains, legumes, beans or with just vegetables. They need not take a lot of time to put together. Using what is available to you at the time can hurry things along. Left over rice can be turned into Wild Brown Rice Salad with Curried Dressing (pg. 128). An abundance of cooked lentils can be whipped into Green Lentil and Swiss Chard salad (pg. 132) without much effort. A single ingredient like chickpeas tossed with Arugula Almond Pesto (pg. 156) will be a crowd pleaser.

I have tried to create not only delicious, easy to make salads, but to use power foods such as quinoa, adzuki beans and mineral rich seaweed.

A few extra salad tips to help you.

- Cook extra beans and rice and freeze in portions. Defrost the night before or microwave if you are in a pinch for time.
- Use quick cooking grains such as couscous, bulgur and quinoa.
- Make an extra amount of salad dressing and use over greens for one meal then toss with a grain or vegetables for another meal.
- Add fruit to salad greens. Vitamin rich sliced strawberries, antioxidant blueberries or dried cranberries. Papaya and pineapple aid digestion.
- Make a warm green salad using heartier greens such as kale, romaine and beet greens, then toss with Peanut Sauce (pg. 149). Serve with a

side of whole grains.
- Add toasted nuts like walnuts, almonds or pecans, or toasted seeds like pumpkin, sunflower or sesame seeds.
- Toss cooked legumes such as kidney beans, black beans or chickpeas with salad greens.
- Add steamed edamame (soybeans) or roasted tofu cubes for extra protein.
- Toss salad greens with fresh herbs and serve with a sprinkling of extra virgin olive oil, a splash of Bragg seasoning topped with a teaspoon of nutritional yeast.
- Shred liver loving beets, or antioxidant rich carrots and add to salad greens.
- Grow a garden and feel the earth. If you have just one pot of herbs, it will make you feel good.
- Don't forget to dress up your salads with edible flowers. Calendula, pansies, nasturtiums, oregano flowers or Johnny Jump Ups.

Antipasti Salad page 129

WHITE BEAN SALAD WITH HIJICKI

Serves 4   VEGAN

Hijicki is a thin strand of sea vegetable with a bold taste making this a very hearty full flavoured salad. It is available at health stores and Asian markets. Prepare the beans ahead of time (pg. 58) or use unsalted canned beans if pushed for time.

1 cup	dried Hijicki
4 cups	white kidney beans, cooked
3	carrots, chopped
1 cup	radishes, chopped
1	yellow bell pepper, chopped
2	celery stalks, chopped
4	scallions, chopped
1 cup	Swiss chard leaves, chiffonade
¼ cup	lemon juice
¼ cup	Bragg all purpose seasoning
1 tsp	sea salt
1 tsp	Dijon mustard
1 tbsp	honey or agave nectar
	fresh ground pepper to taste

In a small bowl cover the Hijicki with boiling water and let sit 15 minutes until reconstituted. Drain, reserving liquid to add to a soup stock if desired.

Combine all vegetables together in a large bowl. Whisk together dressing ingredients until creamy and pour over salad. Taste, adding more pepper if you like.

RED QUINOA & ADZUKI BEAN SALAD

Serves 6   *VEGAN*

Red quinoa is vibrant in colour and is a good source of plant protein, iron, potassium, magnesium and lysine.

1 cup	red quinoa
⅓ cup	sunflower seeds, toasted
½ cup	Arame
1 cup each	corn & sugar snap peas, blanched
1	carrot, chopped
1½ cups	Adzuki beans, cooked
¼ cup	scallions, chopped
¼ cup	red wine vinegar
2 tbsp	mirin
½ cup	olive oil
1	garlic clove, minced
½ tsp	ground coriander
¼ tsp	cayenne pepper
1 tsp	honey or agave nectar
1 tbsp	Bragg all purpose seasoning
pinch	5 spice seasonings
	sea salt, fresh ground pepper to taste

Bring 2 cups of salted water to a boil and add quinoa. Cover and simmer over low heat for 15 minutes. Drain and let cool. Cover the Arame with cold water and soak for 10 minutes, drain and set aside.

Toss all vegetables together in a large bowl. In a separate bowl, whisk together dressing ingredients and pour over salad, stirring to coat.

Harmony Dawn Salad Niçoise

Serves 4

This is a colourful salad that you can make as elaborate or as simple as you like depending on the optional additions. Serve with Leek and Potato Soup (pg. 170) and Whole Wheat Herb Baguette (pg. 78).

2-3 tbsp	olive oil
3	sweet potatoes, cut into wedges
3-4	medium size beets, peeled & cut into wedges
2 cups	green beans, steamed until just tender
4	eggs, hard boiled, cut into wedges
1 cup	black kalamata olives
1-2 cups	cherry tomatoes
4 cups	combination of mixed greens, arugula & spinach
½ cup mixed	chopped Italian parsley, fresh dill & chives
	coarse sea salt & fresh ground pepper
1 cup or so	Lemon Parsley Dressing (pg. 147)
Optional:	1 cup tofu, cut into 1 inch pieces and grilled
	1 small can artichoke hearts, quartered
	1 cup hearts of palm, cut into 1 inch pieces
	1 bunch asparagus spears, roasted

Pre-heat oven to 425° F. Place beets in a piece of foil and sprinkle with olive oil, a touch of coarse salt and pepper. Fold foil over beets and place on the baking sheet. Roast in oven for about 45 minutes until tender. Be careful when you open the foil as steam will escape.

Meanwhile toss the sweet potatoes with oil, coarse salt and pepper and place on another baking tray 15 minutes into the cooking of the beets. Turn once during cooking and remove when just tender.

To assemble the salad you can use a large platter or individual plates. Begin with the lettuce greens in the middle and then group the vegetables around the platter/plate in a colourful manner. Pour the dressing lightly over the salad and sprinkle with the fresh herbs. Serve any remaining dressing on the side.

BEET FETA HAZELNUT SALAD

Serves 8

This is a beautiful purple salad interspersed with mineral rich beet greens, creamy feta and nutrient rich sweet hazelnuts.

4 cups	beets, peeled & chopped into ½ squares
1¼ cups	hazelnuts, minced
1 large	shallot, sliced
4 cups	beet greens, chiffonade
½ cup	feta cheese
3 tbsp	pear vinegar
½ tsp	Dijon mustard
½ tsp	sea salt
6 tbsp	walnut oil
4 tbsp	canola oil
2	Anjou pears, peeled & chopped, optional

Steam the beets until just tender about 15 minutes. Toast hazelnuts in a small frying pan until fragrant, remove skins and set aside.

In a small bowl whisk together the vinegar, mustard, salt and oils until creamy. Combine beets, shallot, beet greens and feta together in a large bowl and toss with dressing to coat. Sprinkle hazelnuts over salad and serve.

Choose to shower instead of taking a bath.
A 5 minute shower uses up to 50% less water than a bath.

MANGO & CABBAGE SALAD

Serves 4

Crunchy and sweet this salad is a refreshing addition to any summer barbeque. It is best to wait until the very last minute to toss the salad so the cabbage remains crispy.

Salad
2 cups	purple cabbage, shredded
2 cups	green cabbage, shredded
1 cup	cucumber, peeled, cut into cubes
1 cup	red pepper, cut into cubes
1	firm mango, peeled, cut into cubes
2-3	scallions, thinly sliced
½ bunch	fresh coriander, chopped

Dressing
2	garlic cloves, minced
2	limes, juiced, about 4 tbsp
2 tbsp	honey
½ tsp	sea salt
½ cup	olive oil
½ tsp	fresh ground pepper
1 tsp	ground cumin
1 tbsp	plain yogurt

In a large bowl, toss all the vegetables, mango and coriander. In a small bowl, combine the garlic, lime, honey and salt. Add remaining ingredients and whisk until creamy. Taste and adjust seasonings if necessary. Pour dressing over salad prior to serving and toss until all vegetables are coated with the dressing.

ROASTED PUMPKIN LENTIL SALAD

Serves 6   ᵛEGAₙ

This is a festive occasion salad that is perfect in the autumn when small pumpkins are sweet and plentiful. I like to make extra dressing to sprinkle over the top as it just tastes so sweet and yummy.

2 tbsp	olive oil
1 small	pumpkin, peeled & cut into 1 inch pieces
1 large	yellow onion, quartered
¼ tsp	dried sage
6 cups	green lentils, cooked, about 3½ cups dried
	see legumes (pg. 58) on cooking method
1 tbsp	grain Dijon mustard
2 tbsp	apple cider vinegar
2 tbsp	pear vinegar
2 tbsp	honey
2 cups	red & green Swiss chard, chiffonade
¾ cup	walnuts, toasted & chopped
	coarse sea salt & fresh ground pepper

Pre-heat oven to 350° F and lightly oil a baking sheet. In a bowl toss pumpkin, onion and sage together with the oil and sprinkle with coarse salt and pepper. Roast in the oven for about 20 minutes until the pumpkin is just tender.

Meanwhile prepare salad. Whisk together the mustard, vinegars, honey, salt and pepper to taste. Toss in the cooked lentils and chards. To serve, place a cup of lentils on each plate and top with the roasted pumpkin and extra dressing if desired.

SIMPLE BEAN & SPINACH SALAD

Serves 2   VEGAN

This salad is very simple to prepare and fast. For a variation substitute fresh dandelion leaves for the spinach leaves and add 1 cup of soaked Arame.

I prefer to use dried beans that have been soaked and boiled rather than canned, see legumes (pg. 58). They are more economical, there are no cans to throw away and they contain no added sodium. Make a large batch and freeze in small portions.

2 cups	white kidney beans, cooked, 1–19 oz can
2 cups	fresh spinach, chopped
1 cup	red cabbage, thinly sliced
1 cup	edamame beans, cooked
½ cup	yellow pepper, minced
2 small	garlic cloves, minced, about 1 tsp
1 tbsp	Bragg all purpose seasoning
2 tsp	lemon juice
¼ tsp	dried chili flakes
½ tsp	sesame oil
5 tbsp	vegetable oil
2 tbsp	scallions, minced fine
1 tsp	dulse flakes, or to taste

In a medium sized bowl whisk together garlic, Bragg seasoning, lemon juice, chili flakes, sesame oil and vegetable oil until creamy. Add beans and stir to coat beans with dressing. Stir in remaining vegetables and sprinkle with the scallions and dulse flakes.

INDONESIAN GADO GADO SALAD

Serves 6   VEGAN

This is a classic Indonesian layered salad served with a warm spicy peanut sauce over the top. Serve with a side of brown rice. Substitute tofu or seitan if you prefer. Omit eggs if vegan.

Salad

1 pkg	tempeh, cut into ½ inch thin strips
2 tbsp	Bragg all purpose seasoning
4 cups	Napa cabbage, shredded
2 cups	spinach greens, shredded
2 cups	French green beans, steamed whole
2 cups	Yukon gold potatoes, cut into slices & steamed
2 cups	carrots, cut into sticks & lightly steamed
½	English cucumber, peeled & sliced into rounds
1 cup	mung bean sprouts
3	hardboiled eggs, sliced
1 cup	cherry tomatoes, left whole
1 cup	red pepper, cut into sticks
	fresh coriander & toasted peanuts for garnish

Pre-heat oven to 350º F and lightly oil a baking sheet. Toss the tempeh with the Bragg's and bake in the oven until crisp, about 15 minutes.

To assemble the salad, begin with the napa and spinach and then layer the vegetables and tempeh on top ending with the bean sprouts. Reserve the eggs and tomatoes for garnish around the outside. Pour sauce over the salad and sprinkle with the coriander and toasted peanuts.

Sauce

2 inch piece	fresh ginger, peeled
4 large	garlic cloves, peeled
2 small	fresh Thai red chilies, seeded
2 medium	red onions, quartered
1½ cups	peanuts, toasted
2 tbsp	peanut oil
1 can	coconut milk
½ cup	stock (pg. 166)
5 tbsp	tamari
½ tsp	sea salt
1 tbsp	mirin
1 tbsp	tamarind paste
½	lime, juiced or to taste
½ cup	peanut butter

To make the sauce, purée the ginger, garlic, chilies and onion in a food processor until they form a paste. Remove and add the toasted peanuts to the processor and pulverize until fine. Heat oil in a wok over medium high heat and fry the onion mixture until fragrant.

Add the remaining ingredients and cook over a low heat, stirring frequently until sauce thickens. Taste and adjust seasonings.

Pictured on opening chapter..........page 113

GRILLED VEGETABLE SALAD

Serves 6　　　　　　　　　ᵥEGAₙ

Serve as a side salad to Crispy Tofu Steaks (pg. 221) topped with
Coriander Tahini Sauce (pg. 150) and steamy brown rice.

	olive oil
1	young eggplant, sliced into 1 inch circular pieces
1 large	red onion, as above
1	red pepper, left whole *
1	green pepper, as above
1-2	zucchini, cut into 2 inch long pieces
4-5	tomatoes, cut into chunks
1 head	garlic, roasted and separated into cloves *
2 cups or so	arugula leaves
½ cup	fresh Italian flat leaf parsley, chopped
½ cup	fresh basil, chopped
	coarse sea salt & fresh ground pepper

*See glossary on roasting peppers and roasting garlic

Heat the barbeque and brush the grill lightly with oil. Brush eggplant,
onion, and zucchini with oil and sprinkle with salt and pepper. Place on
the grill and cook until just tender. Repeat on the other side. Some of
the vegetables will take longer than others to cook.

Transfer the vegetables to a cutting board and slice them into big
chunks and place in a large bowl. Add remaining ingredients and toss
with a sprinkling of salt, pepper and a touch of olive oil. Serve warm or
at room temperature.

BLACK BEAN & DULSE SALAD

Serves 2   *VEGAN*

Crunchy vegetables mixed with hearty black beans in a savoury dressing, yummy! Serve with Sweet Potato Honey and Cumin Buns (pg. 74) or along side Leek and Potato Soup (pg. 170).

1	garlic clove, minced
1 tsp	Dijon mustard
1 tbsp	cider vinegar
½ tsp	light miso
¼ tsp	organic sugar
1 tbsp	Bragg all purpose seasoning
6 tbsp	olive oil
pinch	fresh ground pepper
½ cup	snow peas, sliced in half diagonally
½ cup	corn, fresh or frozen
1	scallion, chopped
1	carrot, shaved
1 cup	romaine leaves, shredded
1 tsp	dulse flakes or to taste

Whisk together the first 8 ingredients until creamy. Blanch the snow peas and corn by plunging them into boiling water for a minute and then submerge in ice cold water. Remove and drain.

In a large bowl toss together all salad ingredients with the dressing and serve.

WILD BROWN RICE SALAD WITH CURRIED DRESSING

Serves 6   *VEGAN*

Serve this salad with a side of mixed greens with Orange Tahini Dressing (pg. 138).

⅔ cup	short grain brown rice, cooked
⅔ cup	wild rice, cooked according to package directions
3 tbsp	champagne vinegar
2 tbsp	honey
1 tbsp	curry powder
1 tsp	ground cumin
½ tsp	ground coriander
1 tsp each	coarse sea salt & fresh ground pepper
½ cup	olive oil
1 cup	chick peas
1 cup	chopped radishes or daikon
½ cup	toasted pecans, chopped
½ cup	fresh Italian parsley, chopped
½ cup	red onion, chopped
½ cup each	Thompson raisins & currants

Substitute white wine vingegar if champagne vinegar is unavailable.

Combine vinegar, honey and seasonings in a blender. With the motor running, add the oil in a stream until you have a nice creamy dressing. About 30 seconds. Taste and adjust seasonings if desired.

In a large bowl combine rice and remainder of ingredients. Pour dressing over salad stirring to coat evenly. Allow to sit for about 30 minutes for flavours to blend.

Antipasti Salad

Serves 4   VEGAN

As an alternative you can omit the fresh herbs and toss salad with Arugula Pesto (pg. 156) or Spinach Pesto (pg. 151). Serve hot or at room temperature. Omit the pesto if vegan.

	olive oil, coarse sea salt & fresh ground pepper
20	asparagus spears, sliced in half, hard end removed
1	large onion, sliced
3	garlic cloves, sliced
10	Brussel sprouts, quartered
2 cups	French green beans
1	roasted red pepper, chopped * see glossary
½ cup	oil packed sun dried tomatoes, chopped
1 cup	cherry tomatoes, halved
1 cup	cooked chickpeas
2 cups	arugula or baby spinach greens
½ cup each	fresh basil & fresh Italian parsley, chopped, or
⅓ cup	arugula pesto or spinach pesto

Pre-heat oven to broil. Place asparagus, onion, garlic and brussel sprouts on a baking sheet and toss with oil to coat. Sprinkle with salt and pepper and place in oven to roast. Shake pan every few minutes and cook until Brussels sprouts are tender. Add green beans and cook another 10 minutes, or until beans are cooked through and a nice golden brown. Remove from oven.

Place all ingredients in a large bowl and toss to combine. Serve warm or at room temperature.

BLACK LENTIL ARAME SALAD

Serves 2-4   VEGAN

This uncommon combination of ingredients makes this salad satisfying, savoury and sweet all at the same time.

1 cup	black lentils, washed well
⅓ cup	dried Arame
½ cup	vegetable oil
2 tbsp	lemon Juice
1 tbsp	umeboshi vinegar
1 tsp	Dijon mustard
2	garlic cloves, minced
3 tbsp	Bragg all purpose seasoning
½ cup each	red pepper, green pepper & carrots, diced
½ cup	scallions, chopped
1 cup	Swiss chard, chopped
½ cup	Italian parsley, chopped

Place lentils in a small pot with 2 cups of water and simmer for about 15-20 minutes until the lentils are just tender. Drain and gently rinse. Cover the Arame with cold water and let sit for 10 minutes. Drain, reserving sea water for later use (can be added to soups or stews).

In a large bowl combine vegetables, lentils and arame. In a separate bowl whisk together oil, lemon juice, umeboshi, mustard, garlic and bragg's until creamy. Toss over salad and mix well.

Cook seasonally. Use your BBQ in the summer and avoid your oven so you are not overheating your house

Rainbow Cabbage Salad

Serves 4

I love cabbage for its flavour, texture and health benefits.

Salad

2 cups	purple cabbage, finely shredded
2 cups	green cabbage, as above
1 cup	green daikon radish, peeled and julienned
1 cup	carrots, peeled & julienned
1 cup	yellow pepper, julienned

Dressing

½ cup	buttermilk
¾ cup	mayonnaise
¼ cup	rice wine vinegar
1 tbsp	honey or agave nectar
1 tsp	mirin
1 tbsp	tamari
	sea salt & fresh ground pepper to taste
½ cup	fresh coriander, chopped

In a large bowl combine all salad ingredients. In a separate bowl whisk together the dressing ingredients except coriander.

Toss the salad and dressing together and let sit in the refrigerator for 30 minutes so the cabbage softens slightly. Just prior to serving toss in the fresh coriander.

GREEN LENTIL SALAD WITH SWISS CHARD

Serves 2-3 ᵥEGAₙ

Serve this simple salad on a big bed of spinach greens with a side of wild Pacific smoked salmon. Champagne vinegar can be found in most supermarkets, substitute white wine vinegar if unavailable.

¾ cup	dried green lentils
2 cups	water
½ tsp	thyme
1	shallot, peeled & quartered
⅓ cup each	carrot & celery, diced
1	scallion, diced
1 cup	Swiss chard, green part only, shredded
2 tbsp	fresh dill, chopped
2 tbsp	champagne vinegar
1 tsp	Dijon mustard
2	cloves garlic, minced, about 1 tsp
1 tsp	white miso
1 tsp	honey or agave nectar
⅓ cup	olive oil
	fresh ground pepper to taste

In a small saucepan bring lentils, water, thyme and shallot to a boil and simmer for 15-20 minutes or until lentils are tender. Remove from heat, drain and rinse removing the shallots.

In a large bowl combine lentils, carrot, celery, scallion and Swiss chard. In a small bowl whisk together the dressing ingredients and pour over salad stirring to coat all vegetables. Sprinkle with fresh dill and serve.

WARM SPRING VEGETABLE SALAD

Serves 4   VEGAN

A hearty salad with bitter greens that are good for detoxifying the liver after a long winter. Bitter melon is available in Asian markets. Remove the inner seeds and use only the flesh.

1 small	red onion, sliced into slivers
1 tbsp	fresh ginger, roughly chopped
1 tbsp	vegetable oil
1	radicchio head, core removed & sliced into wedges
1 large	endive bulb, core removed & sliced
1 cup	fiddleheads, ends removed & cleaned well
1 cup	asparagus spears, cut into thirds
½ cup	bitter melon, core removed & chopped
3 cups	dandelion greens, chopped
1 tsp	tamari
1 tsp	sesame oil
1 tsp	dulse flakes
1tsp	toasted sesame seeds
	water as needed

In a wok over high heat sauté the onion and ginger in the vegetable oil until softened. Add the radicchio, endive, fiddleheads, asparagus and bitter melon, stirring frequently to prevent sticking and adding water as necessary until softened. Add dandelions and tamari and toss to combine until dandelion wilts. Add sesame oil and toss. Serve sprinkled with dulse flakes and toasted sesame seeds.

Curried Tempeh Nuggets page 237, served with Sweet Chili Sauce page159 ...

DRESSINGS & SAUCES
CHAPTER 4

Dressings & Sauces

Dressings and sauces are an opportunity to turn a simple salad or meal into something exquisite. Lentil Croquettes (pg. 190) wouldn't be the same without the Peanut Sauce (pg.149) and what would Baked Spring Rolls (pg. 232) be without the Chili Dipping Sauce (pg. 159). They highlight and bring out the flavours of the dishes being served.

Vinaigrettes and salad dressings can be as simple as olive oil and vinegar or more elaborate with the addition of herbs and seasonings. Creativity is an important ingredient when making up a dressing, but there is a basic formula that will help guide you in your creation. It is 3 parts oil to 1 part vinegar or citrus. The addition of Dijon mustard will bind the two together better and the rest is seasonings and sweeteners.

Vinegar: white wine, red wine, champagne, brown rice or white rice, balsamic, apple cider, malt or specialty vinegars such tarragon, rosemary or basil. Wine, lemon juice, orange juice, grapefruit and apple juice also work really well. I never use white vinegar except for cleaning as it is too harsh.

Oils: cold pressed extra virgin olive oil is great, but different oils vary widely in flavour and heaviness. Sunflower, safflower, flax seed, grape seed, canola and vegetable oil are all good depending on your final flavour and how you wish it to taste. Specialty oils such as walnut and almond work better with a neutral carrier oil like vegetable or canola.

N.B. Recent research indicates that too much omega 6 in one's diet is unhealthy; sunflower oil is a common source of omega 6. We recommend that you stay current on this subject.

Seasonings: garlic, onion, shallots, ginger, capers, herbs and spices, salt and pepper, fruit, hoisin sauce, soy, Bragg all purpose seasoning, tamari, mirin, marmite, Worcestershire, Tobasco or hot sauce etc. Use sweeteners such as honey, maple syrup and agave nectar.

A few quick tips:

- Use a whisk and bowl, immersion blender, food processor or blender depending on volume and your finished product.
- Use coarse salt and add it with the vinegar. Salt dissolves quickly in vinegar but not in oil.
- To thicken a dressing, use tahini, tofu, yogurt or xanthan gum (a natural binder).
- Add oil in a slow steady stream to emulsify the dressing.
- Taste along the way. If your dressing is too tart, add a touch of honey; if it is too sweet, add pepper. Follow your instincts.
- When making a sauce that needs thickening, use tapioca or arrowroot powder, but always mix them with cool water in a separate bowl first, then stir slowly into your sauce. Bring to a simmer but do not let boil.
- Thick sauces can be turned into a dressing with the addition of a liquid.

Susie Dias of East to West Yoga & Nicola

ORANGE TAHINI DRESSING

Makes about 1 cup　　　ᵥᴱᴳᴬₙ

This dressing can be served over salad greens, grilled vegetables or steamed brown rice. Tahini is ground sesame seed paste and is sold in health food stores, the Bulk Barn and most supermarkets. Pesticides and toxins reside in the skins of all fruit and vegetables so it is important to use organic oranges especially when zest is required.

½ cup	orange juice from fresh oranges
zest	of 1 orange or to taste
1	large shallot, minced
¼ cup	tahini
¼ cup	water
pinch	sea salt & white pepper

Add a touch more olive oil and water and this sauce becomes a salad dressing.

In a small pot combine orange juice, zest and shallots and bring to a boil. Turn heat to low and simmer for 15 minutes until reduced or thickened. Cool.

Place all ingredients in a blender or food processor and purée until creamy.

Use the lids on your pots when cooking saving time and energy by sealing in heat

PESTO DRESSING

Makes about 1½ cups

Use a good quality store-bought pesto sauce, which is low in additives. Alternatively, you could use Arugula Almond Pesto (pg. 156) or Spinach Pine Nut Pesto (pg.151).

1	garlic clove, minced
1 tsp	Dijon mustard
½ cup	prepared pesto sauce
2 tbsp	parmesan cheese, grated
2 tbsp	fresh basil, chopped
1 tbsp	white balsamic vinegar
1 cup	olive oil

Combine all ingredients except oil in a food processor and blend. With motor running, add olive oil in a steady stream until creamy. Taste and adjust seasonings if necessary.

Super Fantastic Red Pepper Dressing

Makes about 1½ cups   *VEGAN*

This dressing was created in one of my cooking workshops by Rebecca and Phil. With a little guidance from me on the basics of salad dressings and the main ingredients they were to use, this is the gem they came up with. All the participants agreed it was "super fantastic" and said it should go in my next book.

1	garlic clove, minced
½ cup + 2 tbsp	roasted red peppers, chopped*
2 tbsp	fresh basil, chopped
2 tbsp	fresh Italian parsley, chopped
6 tbsp	tahini
3 tbsp	white wine vinegar
2 tsp	honey or agave nectar
1 tsp	sea salt
¼ tsp	fresh ground pepper
1½ tbsp	water
½ cup	olive oil

* See glossary for roasting peppers. If using bottled peppers, give them a quick rinse as they are preserved in citric acid.

Using a food processor or blender, combine garlic, peppers, basil and parsley and blend until smooth. Add the remaining ingredients and blend until you have a rich creamy dressing, adding more water if needed. Taste and adjust seasonings.

Honey Mustard Vinaigrette

Makes about 1 cup

This dressing stands up well to spicy mustard greens and arugula. Toss in some hot red radishes, cooling cucumber and thinly sliced mango.

¼ cup	lemon juice
1 tbsp	red wine vinegar
⅓ cup	honey
2 tbsp	honey Dijon mustard
1 tbsp	Dijon mustard
½ tsp	sea salt
¼ tsp	fresh ground pepper
⅓ cup	olive oil

Whisk all ingredients together in a small bowl until creamy and emulsified.

Derek & Margaret Lawrence

Rising Sun Vinaigrette

Makes about 1¾ cups VEGAN

Serve this spicy vinaigrette over cooling iceberg lettuce. Xanthan gum is a natural thickener and can be found in health food stores and the Bulk Barn.

¼ cup	shallots, minced
3 tbsp	fresh ginger, minced
1 tbsp	garlic, minced, about 2 large cloves
2 tbsp	celery, minced
2	radishes, minced
1 tbsp	tamari
1 tsp	lemon juice
½ cup	sesame oil
5 tbsp	rice wine vinegar
3 tbsp	honey or agave nectar
1 tbsp	mayonnaise or nayonnaise
1 tsp	xanthan gum

In a small saucepan, cover the shallots with a ½ cup of water and simmer for 15 minutes to soften. Drain.

Place all ingredients in a blender or food processor and pulse until combined. Refrigerate. Vinaigrette will thicken as it sits.

Install water efficient showerheads and faucet aerators to reduce water and energy usage

ITALIAN VINAIGRETTE

Makes about 1¾ cups   VEGAN

Simple and packed with fresh herbs, what could be nicer on a hot summer day? Toss over salad greens, pasta or steamed vegetables.

3½ tbsp	red onion, minced
1 large	garlic clove, minced
1½	plum tomatoes, seeded
¼ cup	packed fresh basil, minced
¼ cup	packed fresh Italian parsley, minced
1 tsp	Dijon mustard
1 tbsp	honey or agave nectar
¼ cup	white balsamic vinegar
¼ tsp	sea salt
⅛ tsp	fresh ground pepper
¾ cup	olive oil

Combine all the vegetables in a food processor and pulse until minced. Add the remaining ingredients except the oil and pulse again to combine. With the motor running add the olive oil in a steady stream until creamy.

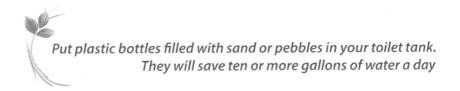

Put plastic bottles filled with sand or pebbles in your toilet tank. They will save ten or more gallons of water a day

GINGER SHALLOT DRESSING

Makes about 1¾ cups   VEGAN

Roasting the shallots brings out their natural sugar caramelizing them. If you don't have time to make the shiitake water substitute ¼ cup of water and ¼ cup of light tamari sauce.

½ cup	shallots, roasted	
2 tbsp	fresh ginger, minced	
¼ cup	rice wine vinegar	
½ cup +	vegetable oil	
½ cup	shiitake water	
pinch	sea salt smidge	white pepper

To make the shiitake water, combine 4 shiitake mushrooms in a small saucepan with water to cover and add 1 tablespoon of tamari. Bring to a boil and simmer for 15 minutes. Let cool for 15 minutes, drain reserving the mushrooms for another use. Wrap the shallots in foil and roast in a 425° F oven or toaster oven for about 30 minutes until soft.

Combine shallots, ginger, vinegar, salt, pepper and shiitake water in a blender or food processor and pulse until smooth. Add the oil in a stream and blend until creamy adding more oil as necessary to create a creamy smooth dressing.

100 Island Dressing

Makes about 3 cups   VEGAN

Silken tofu gives this dressing a nice creamy texture, add more jalapeno if desired. The recipe makes a large quantity, perfect for those big summer barbeque parties. Vegan Worcestershire sauce is available at health food stores.

¼ cup	sun dried tomatoes packed in oil, chopped
1 cup	silken tofu
2 tsp	Dijon mustard
1 large	garlic clove, minced
1 tsp	jalapeno pepper, minced
⅛ tsp	celery salt
¼ tsp	onion powder
1 tsp	capers, minced
1 tsp	Worcestershire sauce
2 tbsp	tomato paste
2 tbsp	maple syrup
juice	of half a lemon
¼ cup	cider vinegar
1 cup +	olive oil
	sea salt & fresh ground pepper

Combine the first 5 ingredients in a food processor and blend until smooth. Add remaining ingredients except oil and pulse to combine. With the motor running add the oil in a stream until creamy and smooth, adding more oil if necessary. Taste and adjust seasonings.

INDONESIAN SALAD DRESSING

Makes about ¾ cup

I like to use this dressing over warm vegetables and Seared Garlic Ginger Sesame Tofu Steaks (pg. 220) with brown rice. Miso contains live enzymes and is very good for your body.

¼ cup	fresh ginger, minced
¼ cup	rice wine vinegar
¼ cup	honey
1 tbsp	dark miso paste
2 tbsp +	sesame oil
½ cup	canola or grape seed oil

Combine all ingredients together and whisk until creamy. Taste and add more miso and sesame oil if desired.

Cathy Mines of Reach Yoga & Andy

Lemon Parmesan Parsley Dressing

Makes about 1½ cups

I love this dressing because it is a beautiful jade green colour. Serve with Mediterranean fare such as Salad Niçoise (pg. 118). With a slight adjustment it can easily be turned into a Caesar salad dressing.

3	large garlic cloves
1 tsp	Dijon mustard
3 tbsp	lemon juice
1 cup	Italian parsley
¼ cup	parmesan cheese, grated
½ tsp	sea salt
¼ tsp	fresh ground pepper
1 cup	olive oil

Combine all ingredients in a food processor or blender and purée until creamy adding more oil if necessary.

Caesar Dressing

To convert to a Caesar dressing simply add the following ingredients to the blender.

1 tbsp	capers, chopped
1 tsp	Worcestershire sauce

Tamarind Coconut Dressing

Makes about 1 cup   VEGAN

You can serve this dressing warm over steamed Asian greens or cold over salad greens. Tamarind can be purchased in block form where you add liquid or already in purée format. Coconut oil can be found in most supermarkets and health food stores.

1	large shallot, minced
1	large garlic clove, minced
1 tsp	fresh ginger, minced
1 tsp	coconut oil
½ + cup	coconut milk
2 tsp	tamarind purée, or to taste
1 tbsp	rice wine vinegar
pinch	white pepper
¼ tsp	ground ginger
1 tsp	fresh lime juice
	sea salt as needed

In a small pot, sauté the shallot, garlic and ginger in the coconut oil until soft. Add coconut milk and tamarind purée and gently simmer until reduced and thickened. Let cool.

Place coconut mixture in the food processor and add remaining ingredients. Purée until smooth. Taste and adjust seasonings.

Reduce water usage and install low volume, high efficiency toilets

PEANUT SAUCE & DRESSING

Makes about 3 cups   *VEGAN*

Peanut sauce is always a favourite. Serve over steamed vegetables, tofu and brown rice. With a slight alteration this sauce turns into a salad dressing.

1 cup	smooth organic peanut butter
1-19 oz can	coconut milk
¼ cup	tamari
¼ cup	rice syrup
2 tsp	sambal oelek
¼ tsp	red curry paste
¼ cup	fresh ginger, grated
1 tbsp	brown sugar
¼ cup	lime juice
4-5	kaffir lime leaves
½ tsp	sea salt

In a saucepan over medium heat, combine all ingredients except lime leaves, water and sea salt. Stir to form a nice smooth sauce, reduce heat to low and add lime leaves, water if necessary and sea salt to taste. Simmer for about 15 minutes, remove lime leaves and serve.

PEANUT DRESSING

¼ cup	tahini
⅓ cup	rice wine vinegar

Let sauce cool completely. Transfer to a food processor and add tahini and vinegar and blend until creamy. Add a touch of water if too thick.

CORIANDER TAHINI SAUCE

Makes about ¾ cup   VEGAN

This sauce is inspired by my good friend Susie Dias who owns East to West Yoga in Toronto. It is a fabulous bright green colour and can be served over lightly steamed fish, vegetables or mixed with brown rice.

1 bunch	fresh coriander, about 2 cups
3	garlic cloves
1 tbsp	cumin
½	lemon, juiced
½ cup	tahini sauce
pinch	cayenne pepper
1 tbsp	honey or agave nectar
¼ cup	olive oil
	sea salt & fresh ground pepper
	water as needed

Add a touch more olive oil and water and this sauce becomes a salad dressing.

Combine all ingredients in the food processor and blend until smooth and creamy. If the sauce is too thick add a touch of water until desired consistency. Taste and add more sea salt if necessary and more cayenne if you would like it hotter.

SPINACH PINE NUT PESTO

Makes about ¾ of a cup   VEGAN

Serve this yummy pesto over grilled vegetables, tossed with chickpeas and tomatoes or spread over toasted baguette slices.

3	garlic cloves
4 cups	baby spinach
¼ cup	pine nuts
1 tbsp	lemon juice
3 tsp	light miso paste
¼ tsp	fresh ground pepper
¾ cup	olive oil
pinch	sea salt

In a food processor blend the garlic, spinach, pine nuts and pepper into a paste. Add lemon and miso and pulse to combine. With motor running pour olive oil in a stream blending well. Refrigerate until serving.

Turn off the water in the shower while soaping your body. Install a low flow shower head with a shut-off lever using 60% less water.

Tofu Tartar Sauce

Makes about 1 ¾ cups VEGAN

This is a vegan alternative to traditional egg based tartar sauce. Serve with Adzuki Sweet Potato Burgers (pg. 200) and steamed fresh corn.

1 cup	silken tofu
1 tbsp	Dijon mustard
¼ cup	pickles, chopped
1 tbsp	capers, chopped
¼ cup	fresh dill, chopped
2 tbsp	fresh Italian parsley, chopped
1 tbsp	champagne vinegar
2 tbsp	olive oil
½ tsp	lemon zest or to taste
½ tsp	garlic powder
1 tbsp	honey or agave nectar
	Tobasco to taste
	sea salt & fresh ground pepper

Using a food processor or blender purée the tofu until smooth and creamy and there are no visible bumps. Add remaining ingredients and pulse to combine. Transfer to a bowl and refrigerate.

Hoisin Ginger Sauce

Makes about ⅔ of a cup of sauce

This sauce compliments the Mushroom Walnut Burgers (pg. 208) beautifully, and can be simply tossed with steamed vegetables.

1 tbsp	soy sauce
⅓ cup	tahini
1-2	garlic cloves, minced
1 tsp	fresh ginger, minced
2 tbsp	hoisin sauce
1 tbsp	sesame oil
¼ tsp	sea salt
	water as needed

Combine all ingredients in a food processor and pulse until smooth. Add water as needed until desired consistency is reached.

Joanne Lowe of The Big Stretch Yoga Centre & Nicola

Spicy Red Pepper Sauce

Makes about 1½ cups   VEGAN

This sauce is yummy served over Black Bean Burgers (pg. 192). Adding the tomatoes and tamari creates an entirely new sauce.

1½ cups	roasted sweet red peppers, about 2
½ cup	medium hot salsa sauce, brand of choice
½ cup	tahini

To roast red peppers, place peppers on a lightly oiled baking sheet and roast in a 425º F oven for about 20 minutes turning every 5 minutes. Pepper should be black. Remove from oven and place in a bowl covered with a plate for 5-10 minutes to cool. Peel off skin and remove seeds.

Cut sweet peppers in half and place in food processor with the salsa and purée until smooth. Add tahini and pulse until creamy.

Tomato Pepper Sauce

3	tomatoes, seeded & chopped
2 tbsp	tamari

Add to food processor with the tahini and blend until smooth.

Satay Sauce

Makes about 1½ cups

Serve along side roasted tofu kebobs for a classic Indonesian party snack. Substitute almonds for the peanuts if you prefer.

3 tbsp	toasted sesame oil
6	garlic cloves, minced
3 tbsp	grated ginger, optional
1 tsp each	ground cumin & ground coriander
1 cup	smooth organic peanut butter
¾ cup	water
6 tbsp	tamari
3 tbsp	maple syrup or to taste
pinch each	cayenne pepper, sea salt & Tabasco
1	lime, juiced
¼ cup	peanuts, coarsely ground & toasted
1 tbsp	fresh coriander, chopped for garnish

In a saucepan over medium heat sauté garlic, ginger, cumin and coriander in the sesame oil until golden. Stir in the peanut butter, water, tamari and maple syrup adding more water if sauce is too thick. Add the cayenne, salt and Tabasco, taste adding more of each until desired flavour and heat are achieved. Add lime juice and serve warm sprinkled with the peanuts and fresh coriander.

ARUGULA ALMOND PESTO

Makes about ⅔ of a cup   VEGAN

This pesto has a lovely peppery flavour from the arugula. Serve over freshly cooked pasta or tossed with Antipasti Salad (pg. 129).

2	garlic cloves
2 cups	arugula leaves, or a small 5 oz package
⅓ cup	sliced almonds, lightly toasted
¼ cup	nutritional yeast, or to taste
½ tsp	sea salt
¼ tsp	fresh ground pepper, or to taste
1 tbsp	lemon juice
1 tsp	light miso paste
¾ cup	olive oil

In a food processor blend the garlic, arugula, almonds, nutritional yeast, salt and pepper into a paste. Add the lemon and miso and pulse to combine. With motor running pour olive oil in a stream to create a smooth creamy sauce. Refrigerate until serving.

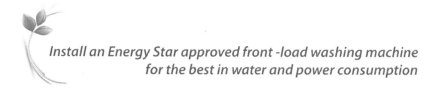

Install an Energy Star approved front -load washing machine for the best in water and power consumption

GINGER SESAME SAUCE

Makes about 1½ cups　　　ᵥᴇGᴀₙ

Ginger is a very powerful herb which helps to cleanse the colon, relieve nausea and stimulate circulation. A little goes a long way.

3	large garlic cloves
4 tbsp	fresh ginger
½ cup	tahini
1 tbsp	honey or agave nectar
¼ cup	rice wine vinegar + 1 tsp
½ tsp	sea salt
2 tbsp	sesame oil
⅔ cup	canola oil or sunflower oil
½ cup	water approximately

Using a food processor with the motor running, drop in the garlic and ginger and mince until fine.

Add tahini, honey or agave, rice wine vinegar and salt and blend until you have a nice smooth purée, about a minute. Keep motor running and add oils in a steady stream until emulsified. Add water a tablespoon at a time until desired thickness is reached.

Mango Dipping Sauce

Makes about 1 cup

Two lively sauces, one sweet and the other spicy hot. Serve with Baked Asian Spring Rolls (pg. 232).

½ btl	mango chutney, I like Sharwood's Major Grey
2	fresh mangoes, ripe but not soft
1 tbsp	fresh ginger, minced
2	limes, juiced
zest	of 1 lime
pinch	sea salt & white pepper
1 tbsp	honey or to taste
pinch	cayenne, optional

Peel and cut flesh from the mangoes. Place all ingredients in the food processor and blend until smooth. Taste and adjust seasonings. Sauce should be a nice blend of tart and sweet.

SWEET CHILI DIPPING SAUCE

Makes about a ⅓ cup

1 tbsp	honey
1 tsp	chili sauce, or favourite brand
2-3 tbsp	water
1 tbsp	lime juice
¼ tsp	dried chili flakes
1 tsp	xanthan gum * see glossary
pinch	sea salt
1 tbsp	peanuts, finely chopped & roasted

Whisk together all ingredients in a small bowl. Taste and adjust seasonings to add more heat or sweetness. Sauce will thicken as it sits.

Baked Asian Spring Rolls with Sweet Chili Dipping Sauce

SHIITAKE SHALLOT SAUCE

Makes about 2 cups

This is a thick rich sauce that goes well with Quinoa Vegetable Patties (pg. 193) or over mashed potatoes. Omit benito flakes for a vegan dish.

1 tsp	olive oil
½ cup	shallots, chopped
1 cup	fresh shiitake mushrooms, minced
¼ cup	flour
2-3 tbsp	tamari
2¼ cups	stock (pg. 166)
¼ tsp	garlic powder
pinch	sea salt & fresh ground pepper
¼ tsp	arrowroot powder mixed with 1 tsp water
¼ cup	scallions, chopped
pinch	benito flakes, optional

In a large pot over medium heat, sauté the shallots and mushrooms in the oil until mushrooms are cooked and fragrant. Add the flour and stir to form a paste. Add stock ½ cup at a time whisking after each addition. Add tamari, salt, pepper, garlic and arrowroot mixture and stir until thickened, about a minute. Turn off heat, add scallions and benito if using and serve warm.

It takes power to heat water.
Switch to cold water cycles to wash clothes.

CREAMY DILL MAYO SAUCE

Makes about 1 cup

This sauce goes really well with Harmony Dawn Tuna Potato Cakes (pg. 196). If you prefer a vegan alternative substitute Nayonnaise, which is soy based and is available at most health food stores.

¼ cup	fresh dill, chopped fine
⅔ cup	mayonnaise
½ tsp	sea salt
½ tsp	lemon zest
pinch	Tobasco

Combine all ingredients in a small bowl and refrigerate until ready to serve.

The bounty of the Earth...

Soups & Stews

Soups and stews can be eaten year round. They are nutritious and satisfying no matter what the season. We often eat hot soup in the middle of a heat wave as do many other cultures in hot climates. They can be as simple as a broth with miso paste and a few chopped scallions or a multi vegetable/bean/rice minestrone with home made croutons!

In this chapter I have included a diverse mix of soups from simple and like Easy Egg Drop Soup (pg. 173) to the more elaborate Sea Vegetable Chowder (pg. 169) enriched with sea minerals. Lentils, legumes and grains all find their way into my soups and stews as do rich antioxidant green vegetables.

Soups and their heartier stew versions are fairly simple to prepare, but there is a formula that will help you to create your masterpieces. First begin with stock of some sort, then layer the flavours and finally, use what is available to you. That's it!

1. Make a stock. Homemade is best (pg. 166), but in a pinch use good quality organic stock cubes. This is done in a separate pot.
2. Start your soup by sautéing the aromatics in butter or oil. These are usually onions (or leeks, shallots), garlic, celery, carrots.
3. Add seasonings and salt and pepper.
4. Add your liquid. This can be stock, canned tomatoes and sauce, milks, wine or juice. Bring to a simmer.
5. Start layering the soup with vegetables, potatoes, cooked rice or cooked beans.
6. Taste along the way. Pull the soup together with lemon juice, Worcestershire sauce, tamari, soy, mirin, wine, beer, cider vinegar or hot sauce.
7. Thicken with yogurt, sour cream, coconut milk, nut butters, tamarind, miso, tomato paste.
8. Garnish with croutons, nuts or herbs.

Quick tips:

- Stale left over bread can be easily turned into croutons. Cut into cubes, toss with olive oil and herbs and bake at 300^0 F for 15 minutes.
- Vegetable scraps can be turned into a quick stock. Freeze them in individual bags as you work and drop into the cooking water when needed.
- For a quick thickener with added vitamins, grate a baking potato into the soup. It will dissolve fast and thicken at the same time.
- Cook seasonally. Prepare corn chowder in summer, beet soup in autumn, root vegetable soup in the winter.
- Keep it simple to begin with and build from there.
- Use leftovers and packaged convenience foods like pesto sauce and frozen vegetables.
- Soups are very forgiving and well worth the effort.

SIMPLE STOCK FOR MAKING SOUP

*The yield for this is about
9 cups of stock*   VEGAN

This is a very simple guide to the making of a stock or broth. You can throw what ever you like into a stock keeping in mind the final outcome of your soup. Certain vegetables are stronger than others and some like broccoli and Brussel sprouts just dominate completely.

1	onion peeled & quartered or
1	leek, white part only cut into chunks or
3	shallots peeled & cut in half
4-5	garlic with skins smashed
2	carrots, peeled & chopped into 1 inch pieces
2	stalks celery, chopped into 1 inch pieces
4	dried shiitake mushrooms
1	piece of kombu sea vegetable
	water to cover, approximately 9 cups

Seasonings - parsley sprigs, bay leaves, marjoram or oregano sprigs, thyme leaves, peppercorns, fennel fronds, celery leaves

Combine all the ingredients in a large pot and cover with water. Bring to a boil and simmer for 30-45 minutes. Strain directly into your soup. For a deeper flavoured stock sauté the onions/leeks/shallots in olive oil for 10 minutes and then proceed with herbs, vegetables and water.

Air dry your clothes instead of using a clothes dryer

SPRING REVITALIZING SOUP

Serves 8

VEGAN

Spring's arrival herald's renewal and healing bringing with it the spirited vegetables that come our way after the long winter. Serve with warm toasted Crispy Pita Chips (pg. 235).

3 tbsp	olive oil
2	leeks, white part only, chopped
6	garlic cloves, minced
2½ cups	asparagus, chopped
1½ cups	radishes, chopped
1½ cups	carrots, chopped
2 cups	white potatoes, grated
1 tsp each	sea salt & fresh ground pepper
1-28 oz can	diced tomatoes
1-19 oz can	white kidney beans, 2 cups
7 cups appox	stock (pg. 166)
2	bay leaves
¼ cup	fresh tarragon or 2 tbsp dried
¼ cup	fresh basil or 2 tbsp dried
1 tbsp	fresh thyme or 1 tsp dried
1 bunch	fresh watercress chopped

In a large pot over medium high heat sauté the leeks and garlic in the oil until soft. Add all the vegetables, salt and pepper and cook for about 2 minutes. Add the tomatoes, beans, stock, bay leaves and simmer until the vegetables are tender, about 15 minutes. Stir in the herbs and watercress, taste and adjust seasonings to your taste.

Hearty Green Split Pea & Kale Soup

Serves 10   VEGAN

This soup is satisfying and "moreish"- you just want to keep on eating.
Omit butter if vegan.

3 cups	dried green split peas, washed well & soaked for an hour or overnight
2 tbsp each	olive oil & salted butter
2 cups each	onions, carrots & celery, diced
4	large garlic cloves, chopped
2 cups	potatoes, diced
2 tsp	sweet paprika
2 tsp	sea salt
1 tsp	fresh ground pepper
2	bay leaves
2 tsp each	dried thyme, dried marjoram & dried rosemary
10 -12 cups	stock (pg. 166)
2 tbsp	tamari
2 tbsp	cooking sherry
3 cups	fresh kale, chopped, hard stems removed
½ cup	fresh Italian parsley, chopped + for garnish

In a large pot over medium heat, sauté the onions, celery and carrots
in the butter and oil until onion is soft. Add garlic, potatoes and spices
and cook a couple more minutes. Drain and rinse the peas and stir into
the pot. Add the stock and bring to a boil, reduce heat and simmer
for about an 1½ hours or until the peas have broken down. Stir in
remaining ingredients and serve sprinkled with extra parsley.

SEA VEGETABLE CHOWDER

Serves 6

$\mathcal{VEGAN}$

This soup is a chunky creamy chowder with a distinct "sea" taste.

3 tbsp	olive oil
1½ cups	onions, chopped, about 2 medium
2 stalks	celery, chopped
2 tbsp	garlic, chopped
1 cup each	butternut squash & potato cut into ½ inch cubes
1 tsp	sea salt
½ tsp	fresh ground pepper
⅓ cup	dulse flakes
2 tbsp	nori, minced
½ tsp	dried oregano
1 tsp	dried thyme
4 - 6 cups	stock (pg. 166)
1½ cups	diced tomatoes
1½ cups	corn, fresh or frozen
½ cup	red pepper, chopped
1½ tbsp	tamari
1½ tsp	sherry vinegar
¾ cup	milk or soy milk
½ cup	fresh Italian parsley, chopped for garnish

In a large pot over medium heat, cook the onions, celery, garlic, squash, potato, salt and pepper in the oil until onions soften. Add the dulse, nori, oregano, thyme, stock and tomatoes and simmer until vegetables are tender. Add remaining ingredients and stir until heated through. Sprinkle with parsley when serving.

LEEK & POTATO SOUP

Serves 6   *VEGAN*

This is a lovely light creamy soup, made without dairy. It is easy and super fast to prepare. If you use organic stock cubes versus making your own stock, preparation time is cut in half. Omit butter and use vegetarian Worcestershire sauce if vegan.

2 tbsp	olive oil
2 tbsp	unsalted butter
1 bunch	leeks, white part only, chopped, about 3 cups
3 large	garlic cloves, minced
4	Yukon gold potatoes, diced, about 3½ cups
	sea salt & fresh ground pepper
1 tbsp	apple cider vinegar
2 tsp	Worcestershire sauce
	dash Tabasco sauce
	stock to cover (pg. 166)

In a large pot over medium high heat, sauté the leeks and garlic in the butter and oil until soft. Add potatoes, salt and pepper and cook another minute or two, stirring frequently to prevent sticking.

Add stock to cover and simmer until potatoes are soft. Using an immersion blender purée soup until smooth and creamy. Add remaining seasonings, taste and adjust if necessary. Serve warm with a dollop of sour cream and a chive sprig for garnish.

Don't use the "heat" cycle on your dishwasher to save on power

PASTA DE FAGEOLI SOUP

Serves 8-10

There are many versions of this popular soup but all include the basic ingredients which are beans, pasta, tomatoes and herbs. Lentil pasta is available at specialty stores, substitute any small pasta if you can't find.

3 tbsp	olive oil
2	large onions, chopped
2	garlic cloves, chopped
1 cup	celery, chopped
4	carrots, sliced into half moons
1-28 oz can	diced tomatoes
	stock to cover (pg. 166)
2 tsp	dried thyme
2 tsp	dried basil
1 tsp	dried oregano
½ tsp	chili flakes or to taste
1 tsp each	sea salt & fresh ground pepper
2 cups	cooked white beans of choice
½ cup	prepared basil pesto sauce, or to taste
½ cup	lentil pasta
	chopped fresh parsley & basil as garnish

In a large pot over medium high heat, sauté onions, garlic, celery and carrots in the oil until tender. Add tomatoes and stock to cover and bring to a boil. Add the spices, beans, pesto and lentil pasta and simmer for about 20 minutes until pasta is cooked, adding more stock if too thick. Taste and adjust seasonings as necessary. Add chopped herbs when serving.

HEARTY WINTER VEGETABLE SOUP

Serves 15   *VEGAN*

This makes a really large amount of soup and is perfect for freezing.
Serve it on a blistery cold day with Tomato Parmesan Scones (pg. 73).

¼ cup	olive oil
2 large	onions, chopped
2	leeks, chopped
1 cup	celery, chopped
5	cloves garlic, chopped
3 cups	butternut squash, chopped
3 cups	carrots, chopped
1 large	sweet potato, chopped
2 cups or so	green cabbage, sliced thinly
2 tsp	sea salt
2 -28 oz cans	diced tomatoes
2	bay leaves
	stock to cover (pg. 166)
1 cup	prepared basil pesto sauce
1 tbsp	dried thyme
1 tsp or so	dried chili flakes
2 tsp	Worcestershire sauce
2 tbsp	honey

In a large pot over medium high heat cook the onions, leeks, celery
and garlic in the oil until soft. Add all the vegetables, salt, tomatoes,
bay leaves and stock to cover. Bring to a boil and simmer until
vegetables are just tender. Add remainder of ingredients and a touch
of honey. Simmer a few minutes and serve.

Easy Egg Drop Soup

Serves 4

This is one of the fastest soups my husband Andy makes and we often have it for lunch. Kombu is a sea vegetable that is sold in strips. It is a deep green colour and is used a lot in Japanese cooking.

4 cups	stock (pg. 166)
4	dried or fresh shiitake mushrooms
1 small	piece of kombu, optional
2 cans	creamed corn
1-2	free range eggs, beaten
1 tsp	toasted sesame oil
2	scallions, green part only, finely chopped
	sea salt & fresh ground pepper

If using dried shiitakes, break them into bite sized pieces, discarding the stems and placing in a medium pot along with the stock and kombu. Bring the stock to a boil and simmer gently until mushrooms are tender, about 15 minutes. If using fresh shiitakes, cut off the tough stem and slice into ¼ inch strips and sauté in a separate pan with a touch of sesame oil, then add to the broth.

Add the creamed corn, eggs and a touch of salt and pepper stirring until the egg is cooked through and the soup is hot. Ladle into bowls topped with a sprinkling of scallions and a touch of sesame oil per bowl.

Install a low flow aerator on your kitchen tap and reduce up to 50% water flow

MUSHROOM ARAME SOUP WITH BONITO SAUCE

Serves 6 -8   *VEGAN*

This soup is a light savoury broth with healing shiitake mushrooms and mineral rich Arame seaweed. Bonito flakes are shavings of smoked skipjack tuna which are used a lot in Japanese and Korean broths. For a non fish version omit the sauce and add a teaspoon of light miso per bowl upon serving.

1⅓ cup	dried shiitake mushrooms
3 tbsp	tamari
1 cup	dried Arame
1 tbsp	canola oil
1	red onion
6½ cups	cremini mushrooms, chopped
⅔ cup	shiitake cooking water
10 cups	water
1 bunch	fresh watercress, chopped
	julienne of one carrot, optional

Place the shiitakes and tamari in a medium pot with enough water to cover by two inches. Bring to a boil and simmer about 15 minutes. Turn off heat, cover and let sit for 15 minutes. Set aside until cooled. Remove from pot, cut off stems and chop. Retain cooking water.

Place Arame in a small bowl and cover with cold water. Let stand five minutes and then drain. In a large pot over medium high heat sauté the onion in the oil until soft. Add the cremini mushrooms and cook until golden brown. Add cooked shiitakes, water, reserved shiitake broth and carrots if using. Simmer for 20 minutes to blend the flavours. Stir in the watercress and serve topping each bowl with a teaspoon of Bonito sauce.

Bonito Sauce

Bonito flakes can be found at most health food stores and Asian markets.

1 cup	dried Bonito flakes
4 tbsp	tamari
2 tbsp	sesame oil
2 tbsp	mirin
2 tbsp	rice wine vinegar

In a small frying pan over medium high heat toast the bonito flakes. They will become very fragrant and slightly crunchy. Be careful not to burn them. Remove from heat. Combine bonito flakes and the rest of the ingredients in a small bowl and stir.

The basic building blocks - lentils, legumes, grains.....

CURRIED DHAL SOUP

Serves 6-8   VEGAN

Dhal is an Indian food staple which is eaten daily for breakfast, lunch or dinner. Turmeric is renowned for its anti-inflammatory properties, curry powder creates heat in the body enabling it to release toxins through sweating and kale is an anti-oxident rich vegetable. Omit butter if vegan and use all olive oil.

2 tbsp	salted butter
2 tbsp	olive oil
3	leeks, chopped
4	garlic cloves, chopped
2 cups	carrots, chopped
1 tsp	sea salt
3 tsp	curry powder
3 tsp	cumin powder
1 tsp	garam masala
⅛ tsp	cayenne powder
1½ tsp	turmeric
1-2 tsp	sea salt
2 cups	red lentils, washed well
8 cups	water or stock, approximately (pg. 166)
2 cups	spinach or kale or a combination
1 cup	fresh or frozen peas
1	lemon, juiced

In a large stock pot over medium high heat add butter, oil, leeks, garlic and carrots and sauté until leeks are soft. Add lentils and spices and sauté for 5 minutes. Add water or stock and bring to a boil. Simmer for 25 minutes until thickened. Add spinach/kale, peas and lemon juice and cook for another 3 minutes.

GREEN LENTIL & SWISS CHARD SOUP

Serves 6   VEGAN

I love lentils because they are fast to prepare and always satisfying. The "meaty" flavour in this soup comes from the miso paste.

3 tbsp	olive oil
1 large	onion, about 1½ cups
4 large	garlic cloves, chopped
2	carrots, chopped
1 cup	green lentils, washed well
½ tsp each	coarse sea salt & fresh ground pepper
½ tsp	ground cumin
5½ cups	stock (pg. 166)
1½ cups	chopped tomatoes
1 tbsp	tomato paste
2 tbsp	tamari
1 tbsp	cider vinegar
2 cups	Swiss chard, shredded
¾ cup	fresh Italian parsley, chopped
1 tbsp	dark miso paste

In a large pot over medium high heat sauté the onion, garlic and carrots in the olive oil until onion is tender. Stir in the lentils, salt, pepper and cumin. Add the stock, tomatoes, tomato paste, tamari and cider vinegar and bring to a boil. Reduce heat and simmer 40 minutes or until lentils are tender.

Taste and adjust seasonings if necessary. Turn off the heat and add the Swiss chard, parsley and miso paste. Serve.

Mushroom Barley Soup

Serves 5, about   VEGAN

The first blizzard of December inspired this soup. Barley is so satisfying
and creamy and the mushrooms seem to hit the spot. Omit butter if
vegan and substitute olive oil.

3 tbsp	unsalted butter
¾ cup	shallots, chopped, about 3
3	garlic cloves, chopped
9 cups	cremini mushrooms, chopped
1 tsp	sea salt
½ tsp	fresh ground pepper
¼ cup	whole wheat flour
⅓ cup	barley
½ tsp	sweet paprika
¼ tsp	celery salt
6 cups	water or stock (pg. 166)
1 tbsp	lemon juice
2 tbsp	tamari
2 tbsp	cooking sherry
½ cup	milk or soy milk
¾ cup	fresh Italian parsley, chopped

In a large pot over medium high heat sauté the shallots and garlic until
soft. Add the mushrooms, salt and pepper and cook until mushrooms
are soft. Add flour and stir to form a paste. Stir in barley, paprika, celery
salt and stock. Bring to a low boil and simmer for about 30 minutes
or so until barley has softened. Add remaining ingredients and cook
another 4-5 minutes. To serve, ladle into bowls and top with a dollop of
sour cream if desired.

ANDY'S UDON NOODLE SOUP

Makes 2 very large bowls

This soup is all about creating a savoury sweet broth base for the vegetables. Udon noodles are Asian wheat noodles that are made with water as opposed to egg. You can purchase them fresh or dried at the health store.

2 pkg's	fresh Udon noodles, (15 oz/400 grams)
4 cups	water or stock (pg. 166)
3 tbsp	Bonito flakes
3 tbsp	soy sauce
2 tbsp	mirin or other sweet rice wine
4	dried shiitake mushrooms, stems removed
¼ cup	onion, sliced
2 tbsp	fresh ginger, sliced into matchsticks
½	carrot, sliced into ½ moons
1 cup	broccoli florets
2 cups	Swiss chard, shredded
10	medium shrimps, skin on, optional
1	scallion, minced for garnish
1	nori sheet, crumpled for garnish

Cook noodles according to package directions making sure to strain and rinse them when cooked. Meanwhile, break the shiitakes into pieces and add them to a medium pot along with the water/stock, Bonito, soy and mirin and bring to a boil. Reduce heat and add onion, ginger and carrot and simmer about 15 minutes until mushrooms are tender. Add remaining ingredients along with the reserved noodles and cook until shrimp are bright pink. To serve, spoon into bowls and sprinkle with the scallions and nori.

Tomato Onion Rosemary Soup

Serves 8-10   VEGAN

Serve this Mediterranean inspired soup with crusty Sun dried Tomato
and Olive Bread (pg. 88) and a green salad topped with Italian
Vinaigrette (pg. 143). Substitute vegan Worcestershire sauce if vegan.

¼ cup	olive oil
3½ cups	onions, sliced
1 tsp	sea salt
4	garlic cloves, chopped
1 tsp	dried rosemary
6 large	tomatoes, chopped
3	sweet potatoes, cut into ½ inch cube
⅛ tsp	cayenne pepper
¼ tsp	sweet paprika
4-6 cup	stock (pg. 166)
1 tbsp	Worcestershire sauce
2 cups	chickpeas, cooked, 1-19oz can
1 tsp	fresh rosemary chopped, for garnish
handful	fresh Italian parsley, chopped for garnish

In a large pot over medium low heat, cook the onions in the olive oil
about 25 minutes until caramelized. They should be a lovely golden
brown colour. Add the garlic, dried rosemary, tomatoes, sweet
potatoes, cayenne, paprika and stock to cover. Bring to a boil and
simmer for 10 minutes until sweet potatoes are just tender.

Add Worcestershire and chickpeas and simmer another 10 minutes,
you may need to add a cup or more of stock at this point. Taste, adjust
seasonings and add the parsley prior to serving.

WHITE BEAN & KALE SOUP

Serves 6

VEGAN

This is a lovely soup for those cold winter months. It is almost creamy in consistency due to the grated potato. If fresh basil is unavailable use ⅓ cup prepared green pesto sauce.

3 tbsp	olive oil
2	leeks, white part only, chopped
1 cup	celery, chopped
4	garlic cloves, chopped
1 tsp	sea salt
½ tsp	fresh ground pepper
6 cups	stock (pg. 166)
1 large	potato, grated
1-19 oz can	white kidney beans, about 2 cups
3 cups	kale, rolled & chopped, hard stems removed
½ cup	fresh basil, chopped
¼ cup	freshly grated parmesan cheese, optional

In a large pot over medium high heat sauté the leeks, celery, garlic, salt and pepper in the oil until vegetables are soft.

Add the stock and bring to a boil. Reduce heat and add the potato and beans and simmer gently until the potato disappears into the broth, about 20 minutes. Add remaining ingredients and gently simmer another minute or 2 until kale is cooked. Serve sprinkled with the parmesan cheese if desired.

CARAMELIZED ONION SOUP

Serves 4

Onions are loaded with fructose, which is sweeter than sugar, when heat is slowly applied to them, it draws out their sweetness thereby caramelizing them. They turn a lovely golden brown colour while remaining soft and succulent. Serve with Rosemary and Pine Nut Foccacia Buns (pg. 80).

6 cups	yellow onions, slivered
3 tbsp	salted butter
1 tsp	sea salt
5 cups	stock (pg. 166)
1 tbsp	tamari
1 tbsp	cooking sherry
½ cup	freshly grated parmesan cheese
2 tbsp	fresh Italian parsley, chopped fine

In a pot over medium low heat simmer the onions in the butter and salt until golden brown and caramelized. This could take about 45 minutes or so.

Add the stock and simmer for another 30 minutes. Stir in the tamari and sherry. Taste and adjust seasonings. Serve in bowls and sprinkle evenly with the parmesan cheese and parsley.

Save water and energy and only use your dishwasher when completely full

CHICK PEA STEW

Serves 6

VEGAN

This recipe is a family favourite. Its flavours blend well together with hints of North African and Cajun cuisine. Serve over brown rice. Substitute vegan Worcestershire sauce if vegan.

¼ cup	olive oil
1 large	onion, chopped
4-5	garlic cloves, minced
2	carrots, chopped
2 cups	button mushrooms, quartered
1 tsp	dried chili flakes
1 tbsp	dried oregano
1 tsp	ground cumin
1 tbsp	Worcestershire sauce
2	bay leaves
1 cup	stock (pg. 166)
1-28 oz can	diced tomatoes
2-19 oz cans	chick peas, 4 cups
2 small	heads broccoli, broken into florets, about 4 cups
1	zucchini, chopped into large pieces

In a large pot over medium high heat cook the onion, garlic and carrots in the olive oil until onions soften. Add the mushrooms and all of the seasonings, stirring to combine.

Add the stock and tomatoes and heat to boiling. Reduce heat and add the chick peas, broccoli and zucchini and simmer until vegetables are tender, about 20 minutes.

MEDITERRANEAN STEW

Serves 6   VEGAN

This is such a pretty stew with bold colours from the beans and vegetables. Cut the vegetables into hearty chunks. Serve with a leafy green salad and Sweet Potato Honey and Cumin Buns (pg. 74).

1 tbsp	olive oil
1 cup	onions, chopped
5	garlic cloves, minced
1-28 oz can	diced tomatoes
2 tbsp	tomato paste
1 tbsp	mirin
¼ cup	white wine
2	bay leaves
1 tsp each	dried basil & dried oregano
½ tsp each	Herbes de provence & dried chili flakes
1 tsp each	sea salt & fresh ground pepper
½	green pepper, chopped
½	red pepper, chopped
1	sweet potato, chopped
2 cups	butternut squash, chopped
½	small eggplant, chopped
1 small	zucchini, chopped
¼ cup	pearl barley
1½ cups	red kidney beans, cooked
½ cup	kalamata olives, chopped
¾ cup	grape tomatoes, halved
2 cups	baby spinach
½ cup each	fresh Italian parsley & fresh basil
	freshly grated parmesan cheese, optional

In a large pot over medium high heat sauté the onions and garlic in the olive oil until tender. Add the canned tomatoes, paste, mirin, wine and all herbs and seasonings. Bring to a low boil.

Add all the vegetables including the barley. Reduce heat and simmer for about 45 minutes or until barley is tender. Add the kidney beans, olives and grape tomatoes. Simmer another 10 minutes until heated through then add the greens and fresh herbs. Serve sprinkled with the parmesan cheese if desired.

Basic ingredients for a great stew.....

Ma Bo Tofu served over hearty brown rice page 194 ...

Entrees

The main meal of the day is a celebration, whether it is in the evening or mid day. It is a time when you can enjoy your family, friends or a peaceful interlude with yourself.

In this chapter, I have tried to give suggestions for creating a well rounded Harmony Dawn style menu, which is flavourful, culturally diverse and healthily balanced. You won't find meat and potatoes with one vegetable in this chapter. The most die-hard meat eaters who have come through our doors, have said how great they felt and that they didn't miss their regular dose of red meat.

Seitan, tempeh, tofu, nuts, beans, grains, vegetables and sustainable fish are the superstars of the menu. They can be featured in easy to prepare, fast dishes such as the Quick Salmon Pasta (pg. 203) or the more involved Lentil Croquettes with Peanut Sauce (pg. 190).

Instructions on each recipe guide you on how to balance the entree with other recipes in the book. Please refer to the chapter on Menu Balancing and Planning (pg. 42) for further tips on how to put together a meal plan. Enjoy!

A few quick tips:

- Plan your weekly menu so that one meal can be turned into another. For example, make extra grains and use them to make Jade Rice Pilaf (pg. 239), Nasi Goreng (pg. 240) or Quinoa Ginger cookies (pg. 277). Extra vegetables can be thrown into a soup the next day.
- Travel through different countries during the week, Mexican Monday with Black Bean Burgers (pg. 192) and salsa. Thai Tuesday with Indonesian Curry (pg. 216), fish Friday with Salt Fish Cakes (pg. 211).
- Buy vegetables with longer storage lives such as potatoes and root vegetables that can be used in a multitude of recipes.

Super Amazing Vegetable Patties

Makes 12, 2 inch patties   VEGAN

Combining protein rich lentils, brown rice and almonds with liver loving beets, antioxidant carrots and seasonings makes for a yummy, hearty patty. Serve with sliced tomatoes and top with Beet Romesco Dip (pg. 245).

½ cup	red lentils, cooked in ¾ cup water with ½ tsp turmeric
1 cup	sweet potato, steamed & mashed
2 cups	short grain brown rice, cooked
½ cup	almonds, ground & toasted
1 cup	carrots, grated
1 cup	beets, grated
1 tbsp	olive oil
1 cup	onions, chopped
2 tbsp	tamari
¼ cup	nutritional yeast
1 tsp	garlic powder
1 tsp	sea salt
½ tsp	fresh ground pepper
1½ tbsp	dried dill or 3 tbsp fresh
½ cup	oats

Pre-heat oven to 350⁰ F and lightly oil a baking sheet. In a pan over medium heat sauté the onion in olive oil until golden. Combine all ingredients in a large bowl until well mixed. Taste and adjust seasonings. Let mixture sit for 30 minutes to allow flavours to combine. Shape into small 2 inch patties and bake for 30 minutes turning once.

Spicy Lentil Croquettes over Peanut Sauce

Makes 24, 2 inch croquettes, VEGAN
serves 6

These are very popular at the retreat centre. They are delicious with a hint of the exotic. Serve over rice noodles sprinkled with fresh coriander and top with Peanut Sauce (pg. 149).

½ cup	dried red lentils
½ cup	dried black lentils
½ tsp	turmeric
1¾ cups	water
1 tbsp	peanut oil
3 cloves	garlic, minced
1 inch	fresh ginger, minced
1 small	red onion, minced
2 cups	short grain brown rice, cooked
1½ cups	carrots, grated
¼ cup	peanut butter, organic
2½ tbsp	tamari
1 tsp	ground coriander
1½ tsp	ground cumin
½ tsp	ground turmeric
2	scallions, chopped
	sea salt & fresh ground pepper to taste

Recipe easily doubles to serve a large crowd for a cocktail party. Make the croquettes smaller, provide cocktail toothpicks and use the peanut sauce for dipping.

Pre-heat oven to 350° F and have ready a lightly oiled baking sheet. Clean the lentils by carefully going through them to check for stones and dirt. An easy way to do this is by placing them on a paper towel lined baking sheet. Wash them in several changes of water until water is clear and not white.

Place lentils, turmeric and water in a small saucepan and bring to a boil. Lower heat and simmer for about 20 minutes or until all the water has been absorbed. Remove from heat and set aside to cool.

In a small frying pan over medium high heat, sauté the garlic, ginger and onion in the peanut oil until onion is tender. Set aside. Combine all ingredients in a large bowl and add salt and pepper to taste. Mixture should be somewhat sticky to hold together. Shape into 2 inch round balls and place on the baking sheet, flattening slightly. Bake for 30 minutes turning once until cooked through.

Clean refrigerator heating coils regularly to maximize energy

SPICY BLACK BEAN BURGERS

Serves 8 -10   VEGAN

Serve these full flavoured burgers with Spicy Red Pepper Sauce (pg. 154) and a side of crisp romaine leaves tossed with Caesar Salad dressing (pg. 147) and toasted pumpkin seeds.

6 cups	cooked black beans (3, 19 oz cans)
¼ cup	fresh Italian parsley, chopped
½ cup	fresh cilantro, chopped
2–3 cups	short grain brown rice, cooked
2 cups	cooked corn
3	carrots, minced
1 large	red onion, minced
1-2	jalapenos, minced
½ cup	oats
3 tsp	ground cumin
1½ tsp	ground coriander
1½ tbsp	chipotle purée
1 tsp	garlic powder
1 tsp	sea salt
zest	of ½ a lime

Kids love these rolled in a wrap topped with sliced avocados and tomatoes.

Pre-heat oven to 350° F and lightly oil a baking sheet. Using a food processor blend four cups of the black beans together with the parsley and cilantro until smooth. Transfer to a large bowl and add remaining ingredients combining thoroughly. Let sit for an hour to develop the flavours. Shape into burgers and bake for 30 minutes, turning once until cooked through.

QUINOA VEGETABLE PATTIES

Makes ten, 2 ½ inch patties   ˅EGA˅

These patties are packed with protein rich quinoa, mineral rich dulse and alkaline adzuki beans. Perfect served with Shiitake Shallot Sauce (pg. 160). Canned organic adzuki beans and left over quinoa make preparation super fast. Use red or tan quinoa, the only difference will be the final colour of the patty.

1 tsp	olive oil
1	red onion, chopped
2	garlic cloves, chopped
1, 14 oz can	Adzuki beans, I like Natures own brand
1 cup	cooked quinoa, red or tan
¾ cup	cauliflower florets, steamed
¾ cup	butternut squash, steamed
½ cup	peas, fresh or frozen
½ tsp	seasoned salt
1 tbsp	dulse
1 tsp	dried thyme
¼ tsp	dried chili flakes
¼ tsp	garlic powder
2 tbsp	Bragg all purpose seasoning
2 tbsp	tahini

Pre-heat oven to 350º F and lightly oil a baking sheet. See glossary on how to cook quinoa. In a small frying pan over medium heat sauté onion and garlic in the oil until soft. In a large bowl combine all ingredients.

Shape into patties, place on baking sheet and bake for 20-30 minutes, turning after 10 minutes. Patties should be steaming inside and crispy on the outside.

MA BO TOFU

Serves 5 as an entrée, 10 as a side dish VEGAN

This is a simple spicy Sichuan meal. Shiitake mushrooms are meaty in texture with an earthy savoury flavour, perfect for vegetarians. Serve over brown rice or your favourite grain. Vegetarian fish sauce is available at Health stores.

2 cups	dried shiitake mushrooms
1 tbsp	tamari
½	red onion, chopped
2 tsp	canola oil
2 tbsp	lite soy sauce
2 tbsp	kecap manis
2 tsp	fish sauce, optional
½ tsp	chili oil, or to taste
2 tbsp	tapioca flour
2 cups	vegetable stock (pg. 166)
2 cups	savoy cabbage, shredded
2 cups	baby bok choy, left whole
½ cup	red pepper, chopped
1 pkg	medium firm tofu, cut into cubes

Place the shiitakes and tamari in a medium pot with enough water to cover by two inches. Bring to a boil and simmer about 15 minutes. Turn off heat, cover and let sit for another 15 minutes. Set aside until cooled.

Remove from pot, cut off the hard stems and slice in half or in quarters if mushrooms are large. Retain cooking water for a later use if desired. In a small bowl mix together the soy sauce, kecap manis, fish sauce, chili oil, tapioca flour and stock.

Using a wok or large frying pan, heat oil over medium high heat and stir fry the red onion until soft. Add seasoning mixture and stir until thickened. Turn heat to medium low, add remaining ingredients and cook until heated through, adding more shiitake water if needed. Serve immediately.

Harmony Dawn Tuna Potato Cakes

8 large patties

These yummy cakes are easy and fast to prepare especially if you use leftover vegetables and potatoes. Serve with Creamy Dill Mayo Sauce (pg. 161) and a large green salad. Pacific Albacore tuna is currently a sustainable tuna choice. Please check *www.eartheasy.com* for up do date information about sustainable fish and seafood species.

3 cups	Yukon gold potatoes, cooked & mashed
2 cans	Pacific Albacore tuna
3 tbsp	olive oil
1	onion, chopped
½ cup each	frozen corn & frozen peas
½ cup	cauliflower florets, chopped small
½ cup	carrots, chopped small
½ tsp	cayenne pepper
½ tsp	garlic powder
¼ tsp	dried chilies
1 tsp	sweet paprika
1 tbsp	cumin
	sea salt & fresh ground pepper

Pre-heat oven to 300° F. In a large frying pan over medium high heat, sauté all the vegetables except the potatoes in 1 tablespoon of the olive oil until soft. Remove from pan and let cool.

Combine all ingredients in a large bowl and mix well then shape into patties. Using the same frying pan over medium high heat, fry the cakes in the remaining oil until golden brown on each side. Top with Dill Mayo and serve.

GINGER TALAPIA

Serves 2

This is a super fast dish to prepare. Serve with steamed vegetables and brown rice. Talapia is a soft white fleshed fish, if unavailable substitute catfish.

2 tbsp	peanut oil
¼ cup	scallions, chopped
1 inch piece	fresh ginger, chopped
2 tbsp	soy sauce
2 tbsp	mirin or other sweet wine
1½ tbsp	sesame oil
¼ cup	water
1 tbsp	arrowroot powder
2 pieces	Talapia

In a small bowl stir together the soy sauce, mirin, sesame oil, water and arrowroot.

In a skillet or wok over medium high heat sauté the scallions and ginger in the peanut oil until fragrant, about 30 seconds. Add the fish and sauce mixture and simmer for about 3 minutes until sauce is thick and the fish is flaking.

Saving water means saving energy and money

Vegetable Korma

Serves 8

VEGAN

A hearty Indian vegetable stew that is creamy, slightly sweet and spicy. Serve over basmati brown rice.

3 tbsp	butter
2 inch piece	fresh ginger, minced
4	garlic cloves, minced
2 small	red onions, sliced into slivers
1 tbsp	garam masala
1 tbsp	curry powder
½ tbsp	cumin powder
½ tsp each	nutmeg & cinnamon
1 tsp	dried chili flakes

Never throw out broccoli stems. They remain crunchy, hold their colour and flavour and never get mushy the way florets do.

2	Yukon gold potatoes, sliced into 1 inch pieces
1½ cups	yellow beans, sliced into 1 inch pieces
3	broccoli stems, peeled, sliced into 1 inch pieces
2 cups	small cauliflower florets
2 cups	vegetable stock (pg. 166)
1 tsp	sea salt & fresh pepper to taste

1	red pepper, sliced into slivers
2 tbsp	cashew butter mixed with ¼ cup water
1 cup	plain yogurt, non gelatin based
2 cups	fresh tomatoes, diced
1 cup	unsalted cashews
handful	fresh coriander, chopped, for garnish

In a large pot over medium heat cook the ginger, garlic, onions and spices in the butter until onions have softened. Add the potatoes, beans, broccoli, cauliflower, salt and stock and simmer until vegetables are just tender.

Add remaining ingredients except the coriander and simmer over low heat until cashews have softened slightly, about 15 minutes. Toss with the coriander just prior to serving.

ADZUKI SWEET POTATO BURGERS

Serves 6   VEGAN

Adzuki or aduki beans are a powerhouse little bean. Mahogany red in colour, packed with protein, easy to digest and alkaline, with a rich earthy flavour. Serve with Ginger Sesame Sauce (pg. 157) and a bowl of steamed jasmine rice. Soak beans for 4 hours then cook for about an hour until soft.

3 cups	Adzuki beans, cooked
3 cups	butternut squash, chopped
2 cups	sweet potato, chopped
½ cup	carrots, diced
½ cup	celery, diced
½ cup	ginger, minced
6	garlic cloves, minced
1	red onion, minced
2 tbsp +	sesame oil
1 tbsp	garlic powder
1 tsp	seasoned salt, or to taste
4	scallions, minced
1 cup	oats

Pre-heat oven to 350° F and lightly oil a baking sheet. Steam the butternut squash and the sweet potato until just tender. Let cool.

Using a food processor, blend half of the adzuki beans along with the squash and the sweet potato until just smooth. Alternatively mash the three together with a potato masher. In a small frying pan over medium heat sauté carrots, celery, ginger, garlic and onion in the sesame oil until soft, approximately 5 minutes.

In a large bowl combine all ingredients together adding the oats a quarter of a cup at a time until the mixture holds together without being too wet. Taste and adjust seasonings if necessary.

Let the mixture sit for 30 minutes to allow flavours to develop and then shape into patties. Bake for 30 minutes turning once after 15 minutes.

FUSILI WITH WHITE BEANS & TOMATOES

Serves 2   VEGAN

The beauty of this dish lies in its simplicity. Use spelt or kamut noodles and vary the vegetables to whatever suits your fancy. For a non vegetarian version add 1 can of oil packed sustainable choice tuna along with the capers. See *www.eartheasy* for information on sustainable fish.

2 cups	dry whole wheat Fusili noodles
2 tbsp	olive oil
1	onion, sliced into slivers
1 tsp	garlic, minced
2 cups	tomato sauce
1 tbsp	capers
1 cup	white wine
1 cup	white kidney beans, cooked
½ cup	broccoli, cut into small florets
½ cup	zucchini, cut into half moons
	sea salt & fresh ground pepper to taste
2 tbsp	fresh Italian parsley, chopped
2 tsp	lemon zest or to taste
Optional	grated parmesan cheese

Always salt your pasta water as it brings out the flavour of the pasta.

In a pot of boiling salted water add the fusili and simmer gently until just tender or al dente, about 8 minutes. Drain and set aside.

In a large frying pan over medium high heat sauté the onions and garlic in the oil until tender. Add the tomato sauce, capers, wine, kidney beans, vegetables, salt and pepper to taste and simmer until sauce reduces or thickens, about 25 minutes. Toss the fusili with the sauce and sprinkle with parsley, lemon zest and parmesan cheese if desired.

QUICK SALMON PASTA SAUCE

Serves 2

I love pasta dishes because they take very little time to prepare and are never the same, as you can use whatever vegetables you have on hand at the time. Tasting along the way allows you to quickly adjust the flavours. Preparation and cooking time of this dish is about 15 minutes, which is about the time it takes to bring water to a boil and cook the pasta.

Kamut spaghetti or pasta of choice, enough for 2

1 tin	wild Alaskan salmon
2 tbsp	olive oil
1 small	onion, sliced into slivers
1½ cups	broccoli florets
½ cup	mushrooms, sliced
¼ tsp	dried chili flakes
1 tbsp	dried tarragon or 1 tsp fresh, chopped
½ tsp	coarse sea salt
pinch	fresh ground pepper
1½ cups	tomato sauce
¼ cup	cream or milk
¾ cup	Swiss chard, shredded

Cook pasta according to package directions. While pasta is cooking prepare sauce.

In a frying pan over medium high heat cook onion, broccoli and mushrooms until onion is tender. Add herbs, tomato sauce, salmon and cream and simmer about 5 minutes until sauce has thickened. Add Swiss chard and cook until chard is wilted about 30 seconds. Toss with pasta and serve.

CREAMY TOFU AND SWISS CHARD STROGANOFF

Serves 4   VEGAN

This dish is savoury and creamy yet it contains no dairy. Traditionally it is served over egg noodles but any noodle will work.

Dry egg noodles enough for 4

2 tbsp	olive oil
1	onion, chopped
3	garlic cloves, chopped fine
3 cups	cremini mushrooms, sliced
½ tsp	coarse sea salt
½ tsp	fresh ground pepper
1½ cups	vegetable stock (pg. 166)
2 tbsp	arrowroot powder
2 tbsp	tamari
⅓ cup	tahini
¼ cup	lemon juice
1 cup	regular tofu, cubed
2 cups	Swiss chard, chopped
½ cup	fresh Italian parsley, chopped
	toasted sesame seeds, garnish

Cremini mushrooms are baby portabellos

Prepare noodles according to package instructions while the sauce is cooking. In a large frying pan over medium heat cook onion and garlic in oil until tender. Add mushrooms, salt and pepper and cook until mushrooms begin to release their juice.

In a small bowl combine stock, arrowroot, tamari, tahini and lemon juice. Add to pan and simmer until thickened. Lower heat, add tofu and Swiss chard and cook until chard softens and sauce is hot. Toss with noodles and parsley and sprinkle with sesame seeds.

LENTILS IN HERB-WINE SAUCE

Serves 2-3   *VEGAN*

This sauce is full of flavour and can easily be doubled to serve more people. Toss in some sautéed mushrooms or add steamed vegetables at the end of cooking. Serve over noodle of choice.

1 tsp	olive oil
1	red onion, chopped
4 large	garlic cloves, chopped
½ cup	carrots, diced
1 tsp	sea salt
2 tsp	dried basil
1 tsp	herbs de provence
1 tsp	dried oregano
1 tsp	fresh ground pepper
¼ tsp	dried chili flakes
1½ cups	diced, canned tomatoes
1½ cups	red wine
1 cup	tomato sauce
½ cup	red lentils, washed well, see legumes (pg. 58)
1 cup	water
1 cup each	fresh Italian parsley & basil
	freshly grated parmesan cheese

Prepare pasta of choice. In a pot over medium heat, cook the onion, garlic and carrot in the oil until carrot is just tender. Add spices, herbs, tomatoes, wine, tomato sauce, lentils and water and simmer for about 35 minutes stirring every so often until sauce is thickened and the lentils are soft. Add fresh herbs and toss with cooked pasta and sprinkled with parmesan cheese.

ALMOND MUSHROOM PATTIES

Makes 24, 2 inch patties VEGAN

These are amongst the top favourites at Harmony Dawn. They are nutty with a meaty texture from the savoury mushrooms. Serve with lightly steamed vegetables. Leftover patties are great in wraps for lunch.

1 cup	almonds, minced & toasted
2 tbsp	olive oil
1	red onion, chopped
3 cups	cremini mushrooms, chopped
1½ cups	fresh shiitake mushrooms, chopped
1 tbsp	dried thyme
3 cups	short grain brown rice, cooked
4	carrots, shredded, about 2 cups
4	scallions, green part only, chopped
½ cup	tahini
1 tbsp	almond butter
6 tbsp	tamari
1 tsp	garlic powder
½ tsp	sea salt
½ cup	fresh Italian parsley, chopped
	fresh ground pepper to taste

If fresh shiitakes mushrooms are not available, use dried. See glossary for details.

Pre-heat oven to 350° F and lightly oil a baking sheet. In a large frying pan over medium high heat, sauté onion in the oil until just tender. Add mushrooms and thyme and cook stirring frequently until mushrooms begin to release their juice.

Allow to cool then place in the food processor pulsing one or two times to mince.

Combine all ingredients in a large bowl and stir with a wooden spoon until well mixed. Set mixture aside for about 30 minutes to allow flavours to blend. Shape into 2 inch patties and place on the baking sheet. Lightly wetting your hands helps with molding, be careful as you don't want the mixture too wet. Bake for about 30 minutes, turning once and serve immediately.

MUSHROOM WALNUT BURGERS

Serves 6- 8, 12 large burgers VEGAN

These burgers burst with east west fusion flavours. Serve with Hoisin Ginger Sauce (pg.153) and a green salad.

2 lbs	cremini mushrooms, stems removed
2 tbsp	olive oil
2 large	red onions, finely chopped
4	garlic cloves, minced
½ cup	fresh Italian parsley, chopped
¼ cup	hoisin sauce
3 tbsp	soy sauce
2 tsp	dried oregano
1 tsp	dried sage
2 cups	oats
2-3 cups	short grain brown rice, cooked
2 cups	ground walnuts, minced & toasted
	sea salt & fresh ground pepper to taste

Pre-heat oven to 350° F and lightly oil a baking sheet. Place mushrooms in the food processor and mince until fine. In a large frying pan over medium high heat, sauté onions and garlic in the olive oil until softened. Add mushrooms and cook until all liquid from mushrooms has evaporated. Allow to cool slightly.

Combine all ingredients together in a large bowl and shape into small or large patties. Bake 30 minutes turning after 15 minutes.

QUICK THAI CURRY

Serves 2

VEGAN

This is a quick, easy and versatile curry that is perfect for a week day dinner. Serve over rice noodles with Curried Tempeh Nuggets (pg. 237) or Seitan Strips (pg. 54). Vegetarian fish sauce is available at health stores.

1 tbsp	canola or vegetable oil
2	garlic cloves, chopped
½ of 1	yellow onion, slivered
1¼ cups	coconut milk
¾ tbsp	fish sauce
1 tsp	red curry paste, I like Thai Kitchen Brand
½ tbsp	tamari
1 tsp	brown sugar
½	lime, juiced
2 cups	lightly steamed mixed vegetables of your choice; carrots, broccoli, sweet peas, red pepper…
2 tsp	fresh coriander, chopped

In a wok over medium high heat, sauté the onion and garlic, in the oil until golden. Add the coconut milk, fish sauce, curry paste and tamari and simmer until sauce is reduced or thickens. Taste and adjust seasonings by adding more curry if you would like it hotter. Add the lime juice and steamed vegetables and toss to coat. Sprinkle with coriander and serve.

Salt Cod Fish

Salt cod dates back 500 years to the time of the European discovery of the Grand Banks off the shores of Newfoundland. It became a traditional ingredient not only in northern cuisine but also in Mediterranean, West African, Caribbean and Brazilian. Salt cod is still widely popular in these regions as well as eastern Canada.

Due to lack of refrigeration, it was necessary for our ancestors to salt the fish for preservation. Traditionally it was dried outdoors in the wind and sun, but today it is dried indoors with the aid of electric heaters. Dried fish has a storage life of several years. Traditionally before use, the cod is soaked in water from 12-36 hours depending on the amount of salt used.

Basic Preparation of Salt Cod

Rinse the cod under running water for a minute or two. Cut the cod into 2 inch pieces and place in a pot along with 4 garlic cloves and 2 tablespoons of cider vinegar. Cover with water, bring to a boil and simmer for about 45 minutes. Taste a small amount of the cod to see how salty it is. If it is overwhelming, repeat the procedure again, only simmer for a shorter period of time.

Capture rainwater by investing in a good quality rain barrel and use it to water your plants

SALT COD FISH CAKES

Serves 4

A variation of this recipe was handed down to me from Andy's beloved mother Beryl. The family's roots are in Guyana so salt cod was used a lot in her cooking. You can find salt cod in most large supermarkets. Serve with Creamy Dill Mayo Sauce (pg. 161), spiced up with a touch of West Indian Pepper Sauce or Tobasco.

1 lb	boned salt cod fish – I use Appleton brand
2 cups	yukon gold potatoes, cooked & mashed
¼ cup	green onions, minced fine
1 tsp	garlic powder
½ tsp	onion powder
2 tbsp	all-purpose flour
1	egg, whisked
½ cup or so	panko bread crumbs
¼ cup	vegetable oil

See Basic Preparation of Salt Cod, previous page.

Drain cod in a colander, remove garlic and let fish cool completely. Place in a bowl and finely flake with a fork. Add remaining ingredients except egg and bread crumbs. Shape into 2 inch oval patties. Dip each cake in the egg and then in the bread crumbs.

In a large frying pan over medium heat add the vegetable oil. When the oil looks like it is rippling in the pan add the cakes and cook turning until all sides are golden, about 6 minutes.

Kong Hei Fat Choy Stir Fry

Serves 4   VEGAN

This is a celebratory Chinese New Year's dish and very easy to prepare. Serve with Seared Garlic Ginger Sesame Tofu (pg. 220), Seitan strips (pg. 54) or Roasted Tempeh (pg. 223) and of course, a big bowl of steamed brown rice.

Wood ears are dried black fungi. They expand to look like black flowers, have a crunchy exterior texture and a mild subtle flavour. They can be found in Asian markets.

½ cup	dried wood ears
1 small pack	dried porcini mushrooms, about ⅓ cup
1 cup	fresh sugar snap peas
2 tbsp	vegetable oil
1 tbsp	garlic, diced
1 tbsp	fresh ginger, diced
1	carrot, cut into matchsticks
½	yellow onion, sliced into slivers
1 cup	broccoli florets
2 tbsp	mirin
4 tbsp	soy sauce
1 tbsp	arrowroot powder
½ tsp	coarse salt & a pinch of fresh ground pepper
sprinkle	toasted sesame seeds for garnish

In a small saucepan cover the wood ears with water and bring to a boil, reduce heat and simmer 5 minutes. Drain and set aside. When cooled cut into half inch pieces. Cover porcini mushrooms with hot water and let stand 15 minutes until reconstituted. Drain, reserving soaking liquid.

Lightly steam the sugar snap peas until just tender, then rinse under cold water and set aside. In a small bowl, stir together the mirin, soy sauce, 4 tablespoons of mushroom cooking water and the arrowroot powder. Set aside.

In a wok over medium high heat sauté the garlic and ginger in the oil until golden. Add the carrots and onions and cook until onion is tender, about 2 minutes. Add reserved wood ears, broccoli, sugar snap peas, salt and pepper and seitan strips if using.

Pour the liquid seasonings into the wok, stirring quickly until thickened. Turn off heat and serve sprinkled with the sesame seeds.

Angela Allen & Nicola

SHEPHERD'S PIE WITH SWEET POTATO CRUST

Serves 4   VEGAN

A comforting classic without the meat. I have used protein rich seitan but substitute tempeh or tofu if you prefer. Marmite is a savoury B vitamin enriched English condiment that is also great on toast or in soups. It is available at most grocery stores in the spice section.

2 tbsp	olive oil
1½ cups	onion, chopped – about 1 large
3	garlic cloves, chopped
1 cup	carrots, chopped
4 cups	cremini mushrooms, stems removed & quartered
¾ cup	green beans, halved
¾ cup each	peas & corn
2 tsp	dried thyme
¼ tsp	dried sage
1½ tsp	dried oregano
2	bay leaves
⅓ cup	all-purpose flour
2 tbsp	tamari
4 cups	vegetable stock (pg. 166) or seitan stock, cooled
1½ tsp	marmite
2 cups	seitan, chopped (pg. 54)

Pre-heat oven to 350° F. In a large pot over medium high heat sauté the onions and garlic in the oil until just tender. Add the carrots, mushrooms and green beans and cook stirring until mushrooms begin to release their juice. Add herbs and flour stirring to cook the flour about 2 minutes.

Slowly add the cooled stock ½ cup at a time stirring well after each addition and allowing the mixture to become creamy, not lumpy. Add the tamari and marmite and simmer about 10 minutes. Add the seitan, peas and corn. Turn heat off and pour into a 4 quart baking dish.

SWEET POTATO CRUST

6 cups	sweet potatoes, chopped
2 cups	Yukon gold potatoes, chopped
2 tbsp	butter or oil
¼ cup	milk or soymilk
	sea salt & fresh ground pepper to taste

Steam the potatoes and mash in a bowl until creamy. Gently heat the butter and milk in a separate pan and add to the potatoes along with the salt and pepper. Spoon over pie and gently rake with a fork to cover the top. Sprinkle with sweet paprika if you like and bake 20 minutes until hot or you see it bubbling.

Place your refrigerator out of the sun in your kitchen

Indonesian Tempeh & Vegetable Curry

Serves 8-10

This curry is an elaborate and celebratory dish. Serve over Thai sweet Black rice with a side of Baked Spring Rolls (pg. 232).

2 pkgs	Henry's Tempeh, sliced into ½ inch squares
2 tbsp	peanut oil
1 large	red onion, quartered
8	garlic cloves
½ cup	ginger, peeled and chopped
2 cups +	peanuts, toasted, (+) additional for garnish
1 tsp	dried chili flakes, or to taste
2 tsp	ground coriander
2 tsp	turmeric
3 cans	coconut milk
2 tbsp	tamari
4 tbsp	dark soy sauce, available at Asian markets
2	limes, juiced
1 tsp	green curry paste
5 tsp	red curry paste,
½ cup	vegetable stock (pg. 166)
5	carrots, sliced on the diagonal, about 3 cups
8 cups each	cauliflower and broccoli florets
1½ cups	broccoli stalks, peeled & sliced on the diagonal
2 cups	snow peas
4 cups	napa cabbage, shredded
1 can	whole baby corn
1½	red peppers, thinly sliced
2 cups	mung bean sprouts
½ cup each	fresh chopped basil & coriander

Prepare the tempeh as per Roasted Tempeh on (pg. 223) and set aside. In a food processor, blend the onion, garlic, ginger, peanuts and spices into a paste. Heat the oil in a wok over medium high heat until just smoking and add the paste stirring until fragrant and cooked, about 4 minutes. Stir in the coconut milk, tamari, dark soy, lime juice, curry paste and stock and simmer over a medium low heat for about 15 minutes to blend the flavours.

Meanwhile in a separate pot, lightly steam the carrots, cauliflower and broccoli to soften slighty. Add them to the wok along with the snow peas, napa cabbage, baby corn, red pepper and tempeh and simmer until the cabbage wilts and peas are bright green and still crunchy. Turn off heat and toss in the bean sprouts. Serve sprinkled with the fresh herbs and additional toasted peanuts.

BARLEY RISOTTO WITH ARUGULA

Serves 4 $VEGAN$

A twist on traditional risotto which is made with Arborio rice. This version combines creamy healthy barley with fresh peas, lemon and arugula. The trick with risotto is being present as it requires continuous stirring to produce the right consistency which is soft and creamy but not mushy. Serve on a bed of fresh arugula greens.

2 tbsp	unsalted butter
2 tbsp	olive oil
2	garlic cloves, minced
½ cup	yellow onion, chopped
¼ tsp	coarse sea salt
1 cup	pearl barley
¼ cup	white wine
6 cups	vegetable stock (pg. 166)
1½ cups	peas
zest of 1	lemon, plus extra for garnish
2 tbsp	scallions, green part only, chopped
3 cups	fresh arugula, plus extra for plating
	freshly grated parmesan cheese and fresh pepper

In a large pot over medium heat sauté garlic and onion in the butter and oil until just tender. Add the salt and barley stirring to cover the barley with the butter mixture. Add the wine and stock ½ a cup at a time stirring until absorbed. Turn heat to medium low and simmer until all the stock has been absorbed and the barley is tender.

Add the peas, lemon, scallions and arugula and stir until heated through. Top with the parmesan cheese and pepper and serve over a bed of fresh arugula leaves.

Black Bean Vegetable Stir fry

Serves 2   *VEGAN*

Quick stir fries are ideal for people on the go. Chinese black beans are sold in jars in Asian markets and they are fermented, salty and packed with flavour. Rinse prior to using.

1 tbsp	peanut oil
1	yellow onion, slivered
1	carrot, sliced in half and then in half moons
1 tbsp	fresh ginger, chopped
2	cloves garlic, chopped
handful	sugar snap peas, left whole
1	scallion, chopped
5	cremini mushrooms, quartered
1½ tbsp	Chinese black beans, rinsed
1 tbsp	sherry vinegar
1 cup	vegetable stock (pg. 166)
½ tbsp	soy sauce
1	cup kale, shredded
2 tsp	arrowroot powder mixed with 2 tsp water

In a wok over medium high heat sauté onion, carrot, ginger and garlic in the oil until onion is tender and golden brown. Add peas, scallion and mushrooms and cook until mushrooms begin to release their juice.

In a small bowl mix together the beans, vinegar, stock and soy sauce and add to the wok. Simmer for a minute or two then add kale and arrowroot mixture stirring quickly to thicken. Turn off heat and serve.

Seared Garlic Ginger Sesame Tofu

Serves 4

VEGAN

You can serve as a steak or let cool and cut into cubes or strips and toss into any stir fry, soup, wrap or noodle dish.

1	block firm tofu
4	garlic cloves, minced
1 tbsp	ginger, minced
3 tbsp	soy sauce
3 tbsp	sesame oil
2 tbsp	water

Slice the tofu into steaks about ½ inch thick and lie flat in a baking dish. Whisk together all ingredients and pour over tofu. Allow the tofu to marinate for a minimum of 1 hour. Set the oven to roast or broil and place in the oven turning once until golden brown, approximately 10-12 minutes.

CRISPY TOFU STEAKS

Serves 4

VEGAN

These yummy steaks have a cheesy flavour from the nutritional yeast.

1 pkg	extra firm tofu, sliced into ¼ inch thick steaks
4 tbsp	soy sauce
1 tbsp	mirin
2 tbsp	olive oil
2	garlic cloves, minced
½ cup	nutritional yeast
⅓ cup	all-purpose flour
	canola or vegetable oil

Arrange tofu in 1 layer in a pan. Combine soy sauce, mirin, olive oil and garlic together and pour over tofu. Allow to marinate for a minimum of 1 hour or overnight in the refrigerator.

Mix yeast and flour together on a plate and dip the tofu to cover both sides with mixture. In a large frying pan over medium high heat, add oil to cover base. Add the tofu and cook until sizzling and golden. Turn and repeat on the other side. Keep warm in oven until serving.

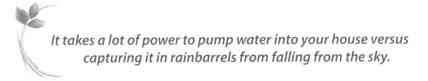

It takes a lot of power to pump water into your house versus capturing it in rainbarrels from falling from the sky.

Sesame & Dulse Tofu Steaks

Serves 4

Serve with Bonito Sauce (pg. 175) steamed brown rice and Sichuan Green Beans (pg. 228).

1	block firm tofu
2	egg whites, whisked well
1 tsp	soy sauce
2 tbsp	black sesame seeds
2 tbsp	toasted sesame seeds
1 tbsp	dulse flakes
1 tbsp	panko bread crumbs
	peanut oil

Slice the tofu into steaks about ½ inch thick and lie flat in a baking dish. Mix the 1 egg white with the soy sauce and brush over both sides of the tofu steaks. Allow to set for about 30 minutes.

Stir together sesame seeds, dulse and bread crumbs and place on a plate. Dip the tofu into the remaining egg white and then place on seed mixture turning to cover both sides. In a large non stick frying pan over medium high heat, add the peanut oil and sear the tofu, turning when first side is brown and crispy. Repeat on other side and serve.

ROASTED MARINATED TEMPEH

Serves 2 - 4   *VEGAN*

Use these crispy, yummy nuggets as an addition to many of the entrees in my book.

1 pkg	Tempeh, I like Henry's Brand
1 tsp	sunflower oil
1 cup	water
½ tbsp	garlic powder
½ tbsp	onion powder
1 tsp	sea salt
2 tbsp	soy sauce or tamari

Variations - substitute coconut milk for the water and add 1 tbsp tamarind paste to the mixture

Pre-heat the oven to 350° F and lightly oil a baking sheet. Place tempeh in a baking dish. Stir together remaining ingredients and pour over the tempeh. Marinate for a minimum of 15 minutes or until tempeh has absorbed most of the liquid. Drain off any excess liquid and place tempeh on the baking sheet. Bake for about 20 minutes until golden brown and slightly crispy, turning once.

Lower your shades/blinds during the day in the summer to keep your home cooler

Yummy White Bean Dip page 243, with Vegetable Crudites

VEGETABLES & SIDES
CHAPTER 7

Vegetables & Sides

Vegetables and side dishes are accompaniments to entrees or lunch dishes. They compliment the main dish with added nutrients, texture, colour and flavour. For example, pairing Sweet Pea Fried Rice (pg. 238) with Ma Bo Tofu (pg. 194) makes a complete dish, nutritionally as well as in texture and flavour.

You can also use side dishes as quick snacks in place of the usual bag of chips or pretzels. Whip up a batch of Mediterranean Bean Crostini (pg. 234) or Baked Root Vegetable Chips (pg. 236) and see how much more energy you have with less fat.

This chapter contains a diverse group of recipes. Although considered side dishes, Nasi Goreng (pg. 240), Pistachio Bulgur Pilaf (pg. 241) and Sweet Pea Fried Rice (pg. 238) can be turned into a main course meal with the addition of roasted tempeh, tofu or seitan. Curried Tempeh Nuggets (pg. 237) is a hit at cocktail parties but with coconut rice and steamed greens, it becomes an instant main course. Sardines 2 Ways (pg. 231) is a lunch time favourite on flatbread but doubles as a canapé for a late night snack. Use your imagination.

A few quick tips:

- Use left over grains for your pilafs and rice dishes to save time.
- Day-old baguettes and pitas work just as well for the crostini and pita chips.
- Stock up on canned beans for a quick dip.
- When nuts are on sale, buy in bulk and freeze.

ROASTED TOMATOES WITH PROVOLONE

In August and September my garden is abundant with tomatoes of all colours- yellow tear drop, sweet orange, plum and big boy reds. I wait all year to enjoy the full rich flavour of a juicy ripe Ontario tomato. Roasting brings out even more of their natural sweetness. Serve them on a toasted baguette, on top of a salad, tossed into pasta or as a topping to veggie burgers.

Ripe summer tomatoes, sliced a ¼ of an inch thick
Fresh garden basil, leaves pulled off
Coarse sea salt & fresh ground pepper
Slices of provolone cheese, optional

Pre-heat oven to broil and lightly oil a baking sheet. Place tomato slices on baking sheet and sprinkle with the sea salt and pepper, one or two basil leaves and a slice of provolone. Place in the middle of the oven and broil until the cheese bubbles and is a nice golden brown colour. Serve immediately.

SICHUAN GREEN BEANS

Serves 8   *VEGAN*

Sichuan is a western province in China and it is renowned for its hearty and highly spiced foods. Commonly used ingredients are chilies, chili paste, ginger root and pickles. Sichuan dishes tend to be dry rather than sauce rich. Serve with Ma Bo Tofu (pg. 194) and brown rice.

4 cups	French green beans
½ tsp	sea salt
2 tbsp	peanut oil
4 cloves	garlic, chopped
2 inch piece	fresh ginger, chopped
2 tbsp	soy sauce
2 tbsp	hoisin sauce
1 tbsp	mirin
2 tbsp	chili oil, I use Manna brand or 2 tsp chili flakes

Blanch the beans for one minute by placing them in a pot of salted boiling water. Remove from heat and immediately place the beans in a bowl of very cold water. Remove and set aside in a colander to dry. In a small bowl mix together the sauces.

In a wok over medium high heat, add the oil, ginger and garlic and sauté for one minute. Add the beans and the sauce mixture and toss until the beans are sticky and tender, approximately four to five minutes. Serve immediately.

SNOW PEA GREENS

Serves 2-3   VEGAN

Snow pea greens can be found in Asian or farmers markets. They are dark green, full of flavour and highly nutritious. Young greens are the softest and most succulent.

1 bunch	snow pea greens kept whole or chopped
1	head of garlic, about 6 cloves, chopped
3 tbsp	sesame oil
dash	dark soy sauce
smidge	water
1 tbsp	sesame seeds, toasted

Toast sesame seeds in a small skillet over medium low heat until they turn golden brown.

In a wok over medium high heat, add the sesame oil and garlic. Stir until garlic sizzles and turns light brown. Add the snow pea greens, soy sauce and water and sauté until greens are wilted. Serve immediately sprinkled with sesame seeds.

Surprisingly, an efficient fully packed dishwasher uses far less water than washing an equivalent amount by hand

Aloo Gobi

Serves 4 as a side dish

This is a colourful Indian side dish that is packed with flavour. I like to serve it as part of an Indian buffet along side Vegetable Korma (pg. 198) and Sweet Potato Puffs (pg. 242).

¼ cup	salted butter
¼ cup	vegetable oil
¼ cup	cumin seeds
2-3 tbsp	curry powder
1 tsp	ground turmeric
1 large	onion, sliced into large pieces
3-4	green Serrano chilies, finely chopped
3 cups	cauliflower florets
3 cups	Yukon gold potatoes, quartered in 1 inch pieces
1 tsp	sea salt
½ tsp	fresh ground pepper
	water as needed

In a large frying pan over medium heat, sauté the cumin seeds in the butter and oil until they crack and are fragrant. Add the onions, curry powder, turmeric and chilies tossing to coat the onions. Add the cauliflower, potato, salt and pepper stirring well to combine all the ingredients. Turn heat to low and simmer until potatoes are tender, adding water to prevent from sticking.

If you wash your dishes by hand, soak the pots and pans first to eliminate excessive running of the tap by scrubbing the dishes

SPICY SARDINES TWO WAYS

Serves 2

Sardines are an amazing little fish. They are an acquired taste just like mackerel, unless of course you live in the Mediterranean. They are flavourful and loaded with healthy omega 3 nutrients. We serve them spread on crackers, on bread, or as a dip with crudités.

Spicy Tomato Sardines

1 tin	sardines in tomato sauce
1-2 tsp	hot pepper sauce - West Indian or Asian
½ tsp	Worcestershire sauce
Optional	1 tsp of minced green onions

Mix all ingredients together in a small bowl until you have a nice smooth paste. Serve.

Cocktail Sardines

1 tin	plain sardines, in oil
1 tsp	Dijon mustard
1 tsp	capers, plus more for garnish
½ tsp	garlic powder
1 tbsp	olive oil
	coarse sea salt

Mix all ingredient together to form and smooth paste. A small food processor works well for this. Spread on crackers or toasted baguette slices and top with additional capers and a sprinkling of coarse sea salt.

Baked Asian Spring Rolls

Serves 6

Spring rolls are always a hit. These are baked rather than deep fried and so are better for you, but doesn't mean they are not absolutely delicious. Serve with Mango Dipping Sauce (pg. 158) or Sweet Chili Dipping Sauce (pg. 159). Egg roll wrappers can be found in most supermarkets.

3 tbsp	peanut oil
½ inch	fresh ginger, minced
2	garlic cloves, minced
3	shallots, chopped
2	carrots, shredded
1	rib celery, chopped
1	chili, minced or ½ tsp dried chili flakes
2	scallions, chopped
2 tsp	sesame oil
2 tsp	soy sauce
½ tsp each	sea salt & fresh ground pepper
1 cup	napa cabbage, shredded
1 pkg	egg roll wrappers
	safflower or vegetable oil
	button or oyster mushrooms, sliced, optional
	red pepper sliced, crumbled tofu, optional

Pre-heat oven to 400° F and lightly oil a baking sheet. In a large frying pan over medium high heat sauté ginger, garlic and shallots in the peanut oil for about 30 seconds. Add carrots, celery, chilies and scallions and cook until vegetables have softened. Stir in sesame oil, soy sauce, salt and pepper. Turn off heat and gently stir in cabbage.

Lay wrappers on your counter in a diamond shape and place about 1-2 tablespoons of vegetables in the bottom third of the wrapper. Roll from the bottom up and as you roll turn in the sides. Dab the top edge with a bit of oil to seal them.

Place seam side down on the baking sheet. Brush oil lightly on rolls and bake for about 10 minutes turning once or twice to ensure all sides are golden brown.

MEDITERRANEAN BEAN CROSTINI

Makes 10 but doubles easily VEGAN

These would be great at a cocktail party. Navy beans are a small white bean with a subtle sweet flavour. Use store bought baguette or make your own the day before from the recipe on (pg. 78).

10 slices	baguette, sliced into ½ inch pieces
	olive oil
3	cloves garlic, finely chopped
1½ cups	cooked navy beans, slightly mashed
2 tbsp each	fresh Italian flat leaf parsley & basil, chopped
1 tsp	capers, chopped
1-2 tbsp	kalamata olives, pitted & chopped
½ cup	cherry tomatoes, quartered
	coarse sea salt & fresh ground pepper
	shaved parmesan cheese

Lightly toast the baguette slices and set aside. In a small frying pan sauté the garlic in about 1 tsp of olive oil until golden. Add the beans and mix together over low heat until heated through. Transfer to a bowl and add the herbs, capers, olives and tomatoes. Spread onto the baguette slices, sprinkle with salt and pepper and top with the parmesan cheese. Serve as is or set in oven and broil for a few seconds to melt the parmesan.

Invest in green technology

CRISPY PITA CHIPS

Amounts are approximate   *VEGAN*

These are simple to prepare and always popular. You can vary the herbs to suit your meal. See Variations below. The amounts given are approximate depending on the number of people you are serving.

whole grain pitas
garlic glove (s), minced & mixed with olive oil
coarse sea salt
fresh ground pepper
fresh Italian parsley, chopped

Variations - fresh basil & sun dried tomatoes, cumin & fresh cilantro or chopped black olives, capers and lemon zest

Pre-heat oven to 350° F and have ready a baking sheet. Slice the pitas in half, pull them apart and slice into triangles. Smear the garlic and olive oil on the rough side of the pita. Sprinkle with sea salt, pepper and fresh parsley. Pop in the oven for about 10-15 minutes or until golden and crispy.

BAKED ROOT VEGETABLE CHIPS

Amounts are approximate   VEGAN

Baking is always preferable to deep frying. Use a combination of root vegetables or whatever you have on hand at the time. The best tool for cutting them is a mandolin unless your food processor has a very thin blade on it. Experiment by adding different herbs such as rosemary, cumin, paprika, cayenne, oregano, basil. The vegetables will shrink during cooking and unless you want all the other vegetables red it is best to keep the beets separate. The chips can burn easily so you really have to pay attention.

> beets
> parsnips
> carrots
> sweet potatoes
> Yukon gold potatoes
> olive oil
> coarse sea salt & fresh ground pepper
> herbs of choice

Pre-heat oven to 375° F and lightly oil a baking sheet. Peel the vegetables and using your mandolin slice them about ⅛ of an inch thick. Spread them evenly on the baking sheet. Do not overlap.

Brush the vegetables with olive oil and sprinkle with salt, pepper and optional herbs. Bake about 30 minutes turning once. Keep an eye on the vegetables as some will cook more quickly than others. If this happens simply remove them from the oven and set on paper towels. Serve immediately.

CURRIED TEMPEH NUGGETS

Serves 2-4   ᴠᴇɢᴀɴ

Serve these delectable little nuggets on top of Quick Thai Curry (pg. 209) or as an appetizer with Mango Dipping Sauce (pg. 158).

1 pkg	plain tempeh, I like Henry's brand
⅔ cup	whole wheat flour
½ tsp	baking powder
¼ tsp	turmeric
½ tsp	curry powder
pinch	sea salt, fresh ground pepper & cayenne pepper
½ cup	coconut milk
½ cup	water
1 tsp	vegetable oil
2 cups	unsweetened medium shredded coconut
¼ cup	vegetable oil

Slice the tempeh into 1 inch pieces and marinate as per Tempeh Marinade on (pg. 54) for 1 hour, drain.

Stir together dry ingredients. Whisk in coconut milk and 1 tsp vegetable oil, adding water if too thick. Dip tempeh into batter and roll in coconut. Place in refrigerator for an hour to set. In a large frying pan over medium high heat, pour oil to about ¼ of an inch. Add tempeh and cook about 4 minutes per side or until golden brown.

Pictured on opening chapter.........page 135

SWEET PEA FRIED RICE

Serves 4 as a side, 2 as a meal

Left over brown rice is ideal when you want to create a meal in a jiffy.
Add more vegetables or top with Crispy Tofu (pg. 221) or Seitan Strips
(pg. 54) to create an entire meal in a bowl. Package them up and take
them to the office or school. See (pg. 62) for information on Rice Bowls.

3 cups	short grain brown rice, cooked
1-2 tbsp	water
2 tbsp	sesame oil
3	scallions, chopped fine
1½ cups	sweet peas, fresh or frozen
2 tbsp	soy sauce
½ tsp	sea salt
pinch	fresh ground pepper
2	eggs, whisked
½ tsp	dried chili flakes, optional

Place the rice and water in a wok or large frying pan and turn the heat
to medium high, stirring gently to combine. When you begin to see
steam, about 1-2 minutes, add the oil and scallions stirring frequently
to prevent sticking. Add the peas, soy sauce, salt, pepper and chilies if
using, stirring until peas and scallions are tender. Add the egg, stirring
until thoroughly cooked. Taste and adjust seasonings if necessary.

*Switch to compact fluorescent lights which use 75%
less energy and last up to 10 times longer
than standard light bulbs*

JADE RICE PILAF

Serves 4   VEGAN

This lovely green rice can be served as a side dish or topped with
Seared Garlic Ginger Tofu (pg. 220) or Curried Tempeh (pg. 237).

2 cups	short grain brown rice
3½ cups	stock (pg. 166)
¼ cup	olive oil
1 large	onion
2 tbsp	garlic, chopped
2 tsp	sea salt
½ tsp	fresh ground pepper, or to taste
1 tsp	dried chili flakes
2-3 cups	fresh Italian parsley, chopped
4 cups	fresh spinach, chopped
2	scallions, chopped
Variations:	add broccoli, peas, cilantro, chives

In a large pot bring rice and stock to a boil and simmer partially
covered until rice is tender, about 40 minutes. In a small frying pan
over medium heat sauté the onion and garlic in 2 tablespoons of oil
until tender, set aside. Lightly steam the spinach for about 30 seconds
to soften.

Transfer rice to a bowl and stir in all ingredients until fully combined.
Sprinkle with remaining oil.

HARMONY DAWN NASI GORENG

Serves 2 as a main,
4 as a starter

VEGAN

Basically an Indonesian and Malaysian seasoned rice dish that can be simple or elaborate. Many cultures have their custom rice dishes, Spain has Paella, etc. Serve as is as a side dish or add Roasted Tempeh (pg. 223) or Seitan Strips (pg. 54) for a meal in a bowl. See (pg. 62) for information on Rice Bowls.

2½ cups	short grain brown rice or 4 cups cooked
2 tbsp	peanut oil
4	garlic cloves, chopped
4	shallots, sliced
2 tbsp	fresh ginger, chopped
1 tbsp	sambal oelek
2 tbsp	kecap manis
½ cup	coconut milk
¼ cup	red pepper, chopped
2	scallions, sliced thinly
½ cup	cucumber, peeled & chopped, optional

In a pot, cover rice by an inch of water. Bring to a boil and simmer gently for about 40 minutes until tender.

In a wok over medium high heat sauté the garlic, shallots, and ginger until just tender, add the cooked rice, sambal oelek, kecap manis, red pepper and coconut milk and combine well. Stir in the scallions and top with the cucumber if desired.

PISTACHIO BULGUR PILAF

Serves 6-8   *VEGAN*

Bulgur is wheat that has been steamed whole, then dried and cracked. Commonly referred to as cracked wheat, it is super fast to cook because of the pre-steaming. It has a light nutty flavour which pares well with Mediterranean and Moroccan dishes.

1½ cups	stock (pg. 166)
2 cups	coarse bulgur
⅓ cup	currants
5 tbsp	lemon juice
1 tsp	lemon zest
¼ tsp	cinnamon
½ tsp	sea salt
½ cup	olive oil
½ cup	shelled pistachios, coarsely chopped
½ cup	scallions, chopped
1 cup	zucchini, diced
½ cup	fresh Italian parsley, chopped
	fresh ground pepper to taste
Variation:	substitute orange juice and zest for the lemon and toss in 1 cup of cooked chick peas

In a large pot bring the broth and 1½ cups water to a boil, add the bulgur and simmer over low heat for about 10-15 minutes stirring occasionally until all the liquid is absorbed. Transfer bulgur to a bowl and fluff with a fork. Add the currants, cover and set aside 5 minutes.

In a small bowl, whisk together the lemon juice, zest, oil, salt, pepper and cinnamon and pour over bulgur, tossing to coat. Add remaining ingredients and serve warm or at room temperature.

Sweet Potato Puffs

Serves 6

These delectable puffs are a perfect accompaniment to Vegetable Korma (pg. 198) or served as a cocktail snack at a party.

2 tbsp	olive oil
1	onion, chopped
3 large	garlic cloves, minced
1½ tsp each	cumin seeds, garam masala, sea salt & fresh ground pepper
4 cups	sweet potatoes, diced
2 large	carrots, diced
1 cup	sweet green peas, fresh or frozen
2 tbsp	lemon juice
1-2 pkg	puff pastry, defrosted
1	egg yolk mixed with 2 tbsp water

Pre-heat oven to 350° F and lightly oil a large baking sheet. In a large frying pan over medium heat sauté onions, garlic and spices in the oil until soft. Add the potatoes and carrots and cook until tender. Add the peas and lemon juice cooking until peas are done, about 2 minutes.

Roll out pastry to about ⅛ of an inch thick and cut into large rectangles about 3 inches x 6 inches. Place 1½ - 2 tablespoons onto each square and gently roll up, pinching ends. Repeat until all are done. Transfer to baking sheet and lightly brush with egg mixture. Bake about 15 minutes or until golden brown and puffy.

White Bean Basil Dip

Makes 4 cups

VEGAN

This dip was created in one of my workshops and it won rave reviews from the group. It is a simple light dip that can be used as the base for a pizza (pg. 102), on toasted baguette slices or with vegetable crudites. Substitute sage or tarragon if you prefer.

4 cups	cooked white kidney beans
1	lemon, juiced
¼ cup	tahini
¼ cup	fresh basil
1½ tsp	sea salt
½ tsp	garlic powder, or to taste
½ tsp	fresh ground pepper
¼ cup	olive oil

Combine all ingredients in a food processor and purée until smooth. Add a touch of water if you feel the dip is too thick. Transfer to a bowl and sprinkle olive oil over the top.

Pictured on opening chapter..........page 225

CASHEW TAHINI NUT BUTTER

Serves 6   *VEGAN*

Nut butters are a great way to add extra nutrients into your diet. This butter tastes rich from the nut combination, so a little goes a long way. Use on toast, as a base for a wrap, or spread on a cracker for a quick snack.

½ cup	whole unsalted cashews
3 tbsp	tahini
2 tbsp	lemon juice
2 tbsp	olive oil
¼ cup	water
1 tbsp	sesame oil
½ tsp	dulse, or to taste
¼ tsp	sea salt
pinch	fresh ground pepper

Grind the cashews in a food processor until fine. Add remaining ingredients and blend until creamy and smooth. Adjust seasonings and store in the refrigerator.

Purchase solar garden lights instead of electric

BEET ROMESCO

Makes about 3 ½ cups   VEGAN

This is a lively dip/sauce made of healthy liver loving beets and protein rich almonds with a touch of spice. Use as a dip for crudités or as a topping for burgers. It is full of flavour and a beautiful purple colour.

2 ½ cups	beets, chopped and steamed
1 cup	blanched almonds, toasted
3	garlic cloves
2 tbsp	red wine vinegar
¼ tsp	dried chili flakes
1 ½ tsp	sea salt
¼ tsp +	sweet paprika
½ cup	fresh Italian parsley
¾ cup	extra virgin olive oil
¼ cup	water

Place beets, almonds, garlic, vinegar, chili flakes, salt and paprika in a food processor and blend until smooth. With motor running add the olive oil until combined. Taste and adjust seasonings. Add water as necessary to obtain desired consistency.

Summer's sweetest bounty showcased in the Ontario Fruit Flan page 260....

Desserts

Desserts are fun (in moderation)! I have tried to create desserts that will satisfy all the basic cravings-sweet, chocolaty, creamy, fruity etc. However, I try to make my desserts conform to the minimum requirements of healthy eating. I try to minimize sweeteners and to use alternatives to sugar e.g rice syrup, dates, molasses, agave nectar etc. For the "creamy" factor, I like to use nut or seed butter like tahini. I often include fruit such as bananas and apples, which add texture and nutrients to the finished product.

Desserts are a huge creative outlet for me and are seasonally inspired. Strawberry Mousse Cake (pg. 266) is delectable in early summer when strawberries are freshly picked whereas Peach and Pear Galette (pg. 262) is more suited to late summer and early fall. Chocolate is an exception and enjoyed year round!

How to make your desserts Vegan
Many of my desserts do not contain eggs or dairy. Some were planned that way while others I chose not to use them to see what the results would be. Substitutions for these classic ingredients will alter the texture of the finished product but what could be more fun than playing in the kitchen and seeing what you can come with!

Egg yolks are used in baking because of their ability to bind with fat and water, making an emulsion which holds all other ingredients together. Egg whites can be whipped from their sticky liquid form into a white soft mass, making them a central ingredient in meringues and the lightest of cakes. They can be replaced in many recipes (except meringues). Here is how you do it.

Flax powder, xanthan gum, agar and arrowroot are all excellent substitutions. All of these act as thickeners, gelling agents, emulsifiers and stabilizers. I have found that flax powder and xanthan gum work well when baking with flour as they can bind with the gluten of the flour and help it along. Arrowroot and agar work best with more liquid based desserts/sauces such as Tropical Fruit Pudding (pg. 281) or as a substitution for gelatin in a mousse such as Strawberry Mousse Cake (pg. 266). Commercial egg replacers are available at health food stores. They usually contain potato starch, tapioca flour and a leavening agent.

Milk may be replaced in any recipe with soy milk, almond or rice milk. Butter tenderizes baked goods and helps to make a soft, moist texture. It can be replaced with applesauce, mashed bananas, nut butter, tofu, olive oil and pure coconut oil.

Sweeteners:

At Harmony Dawn, I use a variety of sweeteners each producing different results. They are divided into two groups - dry and wet.

Dry sweeteners include: Sucanat or "sugar cane natural" is the most unrefined. It is dehydrated natural sugarcane juice. It is dark and has a slight molasses flavour.

Turbinado sugar is made from the first crystallization of cane juice. Light in colour and texture, it is versatile and has does not overpower the dish.

Stevia is derived from the leaves of the yerba dulse or sweet leaf in South America. It is 10 times sweeter than sugar. It has an unique flavour and only a ½ teaspoon of powder equals 1 cup of refined sugar.

Wet sweeteners include: Maple syrup is very sweet and will give a maple taste to the finished products. It pairs well with chocolate.

Honey is not vegan but it works very well in certain dishes because it has the ability to be both liquid and solid. It glues things together, like granola bars.

Molasses is the thick syrup that remains after sugar crystals are removed during refinement. It is thick and dark with half the sweetness of sugar. Rich in minerals you only need a tiny bit for flavour. I use for its unique flavour and pair it with other sweeteners.

DESSERTS

Brown Rice and Barley malt syrup are mild in flavour and are excellent binders, since they thicken as they cool. Both contain added vitamins and minerals

Agave nectar is produced in Mexico from several species of the Agave plant. It is sweet with a neutral flavour. It is sold in light, amber, dark and raw varieties.

Dates are one of my favourite forms of sweeteners. Cooked with water, they form a paste which works very well with chocolate and other spicy desserts. The paste can also be dried to crystallize into a sugar.

Apple juice works well as a sweetener in select recipes.

A few extra hints:

- Always use pure extracts. Artificial extracts contain all manner of nasty ingredients. For example artificial vanilla flavouring comes from vanillin which is synthesized from lignin in wood pulp - Yuck!
- Use only organic fruit when zest is required because fruit is sprayed with pesticides and wax. Generally, 1 whole lemon equals 1 teaspoon of lemon zest.
- Sift dry ingredients together and mix wet ingredients together and then combine them.
- Pre-heat your oven and have ready your baking pans, cookie sheets lined with parchment paper, oiled mini muffin tins etc.

No Bake Sweet Avocado Cocoa Tart

Makes one 9 ½ inch tart

This may seem an unlikely combination - avocados and chocolate- but they actually go together very well. Avocados are creamy and contain fat which is an ideal partner for fat free cocoa powder. Add more sweetener if desired and serve with vanilla ice cream or soy ice cream and fresh seasonal strawberries if desired.

Coconut Honey Cheesecake Pie Crust (pg. 91)

3 medium	ripe avocados
1 cup	cocoa powder, sifted
½ cup +	light agave nectar
2	ripe bananas
2 tsp	pure vanilla extract
¼ tsp	grated nutmeg
¾ cup	coconut milk
2 tsp	agar powder

Slice avocados in half, remove seed and spoon out flesh into the bowl of a food processor. Add cocoa powder, agave, bananas, vanilla and nutmeg and blend until smooth and creamy. Taste and add more agave as desired.

In a small saucepan over medium heat combine coconut milk and agar and bring to a low boil. Reduce heat to medium low and simmer for a couple of minutes until agar is dissolved. Remove from heat and add to food processor. Blend until combined fully. Pour into prepared pie crust and smooth top. Allow to cool and set, about 1 hour. Remove from pan and decorate with flowers.

DATE FRUIT CAKE WITH CREAMY DATE ICING

Makes one double 8 inch cake or 9 x 13 pan for squares

Rich with dates, dried fruit and bananas, this cake is hearty and healthy yet it has an air of decadence. It looks beautiful decorated with edible flowers and best of all, it is also oil and butter free.

1½ cups	dates, chopped
¼ cup	water
1 cup	applesauce
2	ripe bananas
⅓ cup	maple syrup
2 tbsp	molasses
1 tsp	vanilla extract
2	eggs, room temperature

Vegan option- remove eggs and substitute 2 tsp flax powder mixed with ¼ cup of warm water. Stir and let sit 5 minutes until it gels together.

2 cups	whole wheat flour
1½ tsp	baking powder
½ tsp	sea salt
½ tsp	cinnamon
¼ tsp	cloves, crushed
¼ tsp	allspice
zest of 1	orange
½ cup each	raisins, chopped apricots & toasted pecans
	edible flowers for garnish

Pre-heat oven to 350° F. Lightly oil and flour two, 8 inch round pans and set aside. In a small saucepan over medium low heat, add dates and water, stirring until dates are smooth and creamy. Add more water if needed. Using a food processor, purée bananas until smooth. Add applesauce, maple syrup, molasses and vanilla and pulse to combine. Add eggs one at a time, blending thoroughly after each egg.

In a separate large bowl combine all dry ingredients. Add liquid mixture to dry ingredients and stir until just combined. Pour into prepared pans and bake for 35 to 45 minutes until cake pulls away from sides of pan and a tooth pick comes out clean. Allow to cool and ice with creamy date icing below.

CREAMY DATE ICING

1 pkg	silken tofu, blue Mori Nu tetrapack
1½ cups	dates, chopped
¼ cup	water
½ cup	maple syrup
½ tsp	vanilla extract
1 tsp	xanthan gum

Prepare dates as per date cake. Using a food processor whip the tofu until creamy. Add remaining ingredients and blend until smooth. Refrigerate for 30 minutes until thickened. Spread over top of one cake and place the other cake on top, rough surface down. Ice the top and sides and decorate with the flowers.

Use a broom, not a hose to clean driveways and sidewalks

Coconut Chocolate "Cheesecake"

Serves 8-10   *VEGAN*

Although it seems like there are a lot of steps in this recipe, they are very easy to execute and well worth it in end. Creamed coconut and coconut extract are available in most supermarkets.

Base

½ cup	melted butter or oil
¼ tsp	coconut extract
¼ cup	unsweetened medium coconut, toasted
1 cup	graham crumbs
1 cup	ground oats

Filling

1	small ripe banana
1 pkg	silken tofu – lite blue Mori Nu tetrapack
1 cup	dates, chopped
¼ cup	water
2 cups	semi sweet chocolate chips or vegan chips
3 tbsp	creamed coconut
½ cup	coconut milk
¼	coconut extract
1½ tbsp	arrowroot powder

Pre-heat oven to 375º F and butter or oil a 9 inch spring form pan. To make the base: Combine ingredients together and spread over the base of the pan, patting down lightly. Bake for 15 minutes until fragrant. Remove and set aside.

To make the filling: In a small pot over medium low heat, combine the dates and water stirring until smooth. Add the chocolate and creamed coconut, being careful not to burn the chocolate. In a blender or food processor blend the tofu until smooth and creamy. Add remaining ingredients and blend thoroughly. Pour into pan and bake for about 45 minutes until set and pulls away from sides. Let cool completely and remove from pan.

Coconut Cocoa Glaze

¼ cup	cocoa powder
¼ cup	agave nectar
½ tsp	coconut extract
2 tbsp	coconut milk
2 tbsp	unsweetened medium coconut, toasted

To make the glaze, combine all the ingredients except the toasted coconut and whisk until smooth. Pour glaze over the top of cake and sprinkle with the toasted coconut.

Watering your lawn uses 700 litres in half an hour.
That is more than the average daily water
consumption of an entire household

CHOCOLATE BANANA CAKE WITH COCOA DEMI GLAZE

Makes one 8 inch double cake   VEGAN

I had an abundance of very ripe bananas on hand so I came up with this dessert and it won rave reviews. It is a healthy dessert which will satisfy your sweet tooth. You only need a sliver and a little vanilla ice cream will top it off just fine.

6	ripe bananas
1 cup	dates, chopped
½ cup	water
1 cup	semi sweet chocolate chips or vegan chips
1 tsp	vanilla extract
½ cup	cocoa powder
1½ cups	whole wheat flour or spelt flour
2 tsp	baking powder
1 tsp	baking soda
½ tsp	sea salt

Pre-heat oven to 350° F. Lightly oil and dust with cocoa powder two 8 inch round pie pans. In a pot over medium low heat combine the dates and water stirring until smooth. Add chocolate, stirring quickly until chocolate is melted. Remove from heat. Mash 4 of the bananas and add to pot along with vanilla stirring until smooth.

In a large bowl, combine dry ingredients. Add wet ingredients to dry and stir until just combined. Pour into prepared pans and bake for 35 to 45 minutes until cake pulls away from side of pan. Cool completely and remove from pans.

In a small bowl, mash remaining 2 bananas and spread over the top of one of the cakes. Invert the remaining cake on top of the first cake and top with cocoa demi glaze and decorate with edible flowers.

Cocoa Demi Glaze

½ cup	cocoa powder, sifted
½ cup	maple syrup or agave nectar
1 tsp	vanilla extract
1 tbsp	soy, rice, or almond milk

Combine all ingredients in a small bowl and whisk until creamy, glaze will thicken as it sits so add more milk if necessary. Pour and spread over the cake until it drips down the sides.

St. Anna's Chococlate Cake

Makes one 8 inch double cake   ᵥᴇGᴀₙ

This is a heavenly dessert, smooth and creamy with a hint of almond. It is named after the talented artist, Anna Luczak, who studies with my friend, Susie Dias of East to West Yoga in Toronto.

1 cup	dates, chopped
¼ cup	water
1½ cups	semi sweet chocolate chips, or vegan chips
1	ripe banana
1½ tbsp	arrowroot powder
1 pkg	silken tofu – blue Mori Nu tetra pack
1 tsp	vanilla extract
½ tsp	almond extract
¾ cup	almond butter
⅓ cup	rice syrup
1 cup	spelt flour
¼ cup	cocoa powder
1 tsp	baking powder
¼ tsp	sea salt

Pre-heat oven to 350° F. Lightly oil and dust with cocoa powder two 8 inch round pans. In a small pot over medium low heat combine the dates and water stirring until smooth. Add chocolate, stirring quickly until chocolate is melted.

Using a food processor, cream together banana, arrowroot, tofu, vanilla, almond extracts, almond butter and rice syrup until completely smooth. Add date chocolate mixture and pulse to combine.

In a separate bowl, sift dry ingredients together and then add to wet ingredients and pulse to combine. Pour into prepared pans and bake for 25-35 minutes or until cake pulls away from the sides. Let cool and then remove from pan. Ice with chocolate icing.

CHOCOLATE ICING

1 pkg	silken tofu, blue Mori Nu tetra pack
1 cup	melted chocolate chips or vegan chips
1 tsp	vanilla extract

Blend all ingredients in a food processer until smooth. Spread over top of one cake, invert other cake on top and ice top and sides. Decorate with strawberries, raspberries and edible flowers if desired.

Ontario Summer Fruit Flan

Serves 8

This is such a colourful light dessert. Use Ontario fruit in season that is firm, yet tender with no blemishes. Peaches, nectarines, apricots, pears, yellow and purple plums, concord grapes, strawberries and raspberries all work well. Vary the fruit to create a colourful masterpiece.

Base

1 cup	unsalted butter
4	eggs
¾ cup	organic sugar
¼ tsp	lemon extract
1 tsp	lemon zest
1¾ cups	all-purpose flour
2 tsp	baking powder
pinch	sea salt

Filling

1 pkg	silken tofu, blue Mori Nu tetrapak
¼ cup	organic sugar
zest	of 2 lemons
½ cup	lemon juice
½ cup	water
pinch	turmeric
1½ tbsp	agar flakes
2 tbsp	arrowroot powder mixed wtih 2 tbsp water
2- 3 cups	combination of nectarines, plums, peaches peeled, cored & sliced

Glaze

1 pkg	clear glaze, I use Dr. Oetker brand, available at most supermarkets

Pre-heat oven to 350° F and lightly butter a fluted flan pan. In a stand mixer or food processor, whip the butter with the sugar until light and airy or about 5 minutes. Add eggs one at a time, blending well after each one. Stir in the lemon extract and zest.

In a separate bowl, stir together the dry ingredients. Add to the wet ingredients mixing until barely combined. Pour into pan and bake for 30 minutes until golden brown. Remove and set aside until cool. Meanwhile prepare the filling and fruit.

Whip the tofu in the food processor until smooth. In a small pot over medium low heat, stir together the sugar, lemon zest, lemon juice, water, turmeric and agar flakes. Simmer about 7 minutes until agar has dissolved; add the arrowroot mixture and stir until thickened. Add to food processor and blend until combined. Turn the flan out of the pan and spread the filling over the top. Allow to cool at room temperature until set.

Place the fruit on the flan with each piece touching the next so that you have no real exposed areas of filling. Prepare the glaze as per package instructions and spoon over the fruit. This will secure the fruit and also prevents the fruit from browning. Refrigerate until serving. Flan is best served the day it is made.

Pictured on opening chapter..........page 247

Peach & Pear Galette

Serves 6

This is a sweet pastry filled with seasonal fresh fruit. Using ready made puff pastry simplifies preparation, but Whole Wheat Pastry (pg. 84) works even better. Top with Honey Peach Yogurt (pg. 282) and a drizzle of Amaretto liquor.

2 cups	fresh peaches, peeled and sliced
2 cups	fresh Bartlett pears, peeled and sliced
½ cup	fresh cranberries
¼ cup + 2 tsp	organic sugar
¼ cup	all-purpose flour
½ tsp	ground cardamom
1 tsp	orange zest
1 pkg	ready made puff pastry
1	egg yoke mixed with 1 tsp water
¼ tsp	cinnamon
¼ tsp	nutmeg

Pre-heat oven to 375º F and lightly oil a baking sheet. In a medium bowl toss together fruit, ½ cup sugar, flour, cardamom and zest. Roll pastry out on a lightly floured surface so you have a large rectangle and place on baking sheet.

Place the fruit evenly in the centre of the pastry about an inch thick. Fold the pastry neatly around the fruit in a decorative fashion. There should be about a 4-6 inch opening in the centre where the fruit is exposed. Brush the pastry with the egg wash and sprinkle remaining sugar, cinnamon and nutmeg over the pastry. Bake for about 25 minutes until the pastry is puffed and golden brown.

PEANUT BUTTER BLONDIES

Makes 24 mini muffins

This is my version of the popular after school treat. They are not overly sweet and will sustain the kids until dinner. Substitute whole wheat or all-purpose flour if desired.

1	ripe banana
¾ cup	dates, chopped
2 tbsp	molasses
2	eggs
¾ cup	smooth peanut butter
1 tsp	vanilla extract
1 cup	spelt flour
1½ tsp	baking powder
¼ tsp	sea salt

For a vegan alternative substitute flax eggs, see glossary.

Pre-heat oven to 350° F and lightly oil 2 mini muffin tins. In a small pot over medium low heat, combine dates and ¼ cup water stirring until very smooth.

In a food processor, cream together banana, dates and molasses until smooth. Add eggs one at a time, blending thoroughly after each egg. Add peanut butter and vanilla and pulse to combine.

In a small bowl, combine the dry ingredients. Add to the processor and pulse to combine. Spoon batter into the muffin tins and press down lightly with a fork. Bake for 15-20 minutes until golden brown. They will be soft but will firm up as they sit.

CRANBERRY APPLE PEAR PIE

Makes 1 large pie

This pie takes centre stage come autumn. The sweetness of the pears, the crunch of the apples and the zing of the cranberries are pulled together with a burst of orange flavour. Anise seed tastes a lot like licorice and is used to flavour baked goods, liqueurs, soups and curries. It is often used medicinally to treat digestive problems.

Pastry for 9 inch double pie (pg. 84)

⅔ cup	organic sugar
¼ cup	fresh squeezed orange juice
2½ cups	Bosc or Anjou pears, cored & thinly sliced
2 cups	Braeburn or Granny Smith apples, as above
2 cups	cranberries, fresh or frozen
1 tsp	orange zest
3 tbsp	arrowroot powder mixed with 3 tbsp cold water
¾ tsp	anise seeds, lightly crushed
1	egg white, lightly beaten with 1 tbsp water
	organic sugar and cinnamon

Pre-heat oven to 375° F and have ready a 9 inch pie pan. In a large pot combine sugar and orange juice and bring to a boil stirring constantly to dissolve the sugar. Reduce heat, simmer for 5 minutes then add pears, apples and cranberries. Return to a boil and simmer about 3 minutes until apples and pears are soft.

Stir the arrowroot into the fruit mixture and simmer until thickened and bubbly. Add the anise seed. Divide the pastry in half and roll out each piece on a lightly floured surface. Transfer one half to the pie plate and trim edges. You can decorate the edge by fluting the pastry or pressing down with your thumb. Be creative. Transfer fruit mixture to the pie pan.

Using a lattice wheel or knife cut long strips out of second piece of pastry and arrange over the top of the pie in a criss cross fashion securing to the edges. Brush pastry with the egg wash and sprinkle with a touch of sugar and a light dusting of cinnamon. Cover edges loosely with foil to prevent burning.

Place on a baking sheet and bake for 25 minutes. Remove foil and bake another 30 minutes. Serve pie hot or at room temperature.

Strawberry Mousse Cake

Makes a 9½ inch pie

This is a cross between a pudding and a soft cake and it melts in your mouth. Serve with vanilla ice cream and chopped fresh strawberries.

Crust

2 cups	oats, ground
¼ cup	honey
¼ cup	unsalted butter
1 tsp	vanilla extract
¼ tsp	orange extract

Gelatin is a thickener that comes from the bones of animals. It is often added to yogurt to make it appear creamier.

Filling

2 cups	plain 3% yogurt, non gelatin
1, 600 gram	pkg frozen strawberries, thawed, drained, reserving juice
½ cup	organic sugar
1½ cups	orange juice
1 tsp	orange zest
3 tbsp	agar flakes
3 tbsp	arrowroot powder mixed with ¼ cup water

Glaze

½ cup	frozen strawberries
	reserved strawberry juice

Pre-heat oven to 350° F and lightly oil or butter a 9½ inch spring form pan. To prepare the crust, in a small saucepan over medium low heat, combine the honey, butter and extracts stirring until butter is melted. Stir in oats and press into pan. Bake for about 15 minutes until fragrant and golden. Remove from oven and let cool.

To prepare the filling, place yogurt in a fine strainer or in cheesecloth that is placed over a bowl. Let excess liquid drip out of the yogurt until you have a nice thick yogurt cream. This will take about 20 minutes. Purée 2 cups of the strawberries in a food processor until smooth, add yogurt cream and pulse to combine.

In a small pot over medium low heat, stir together the sugar, juice, zest and agar. Bring to a boil and simmer for about 7 minutes until agar has dissolved. Stir in the arrowroot mixture until thickened. Add to food processor and pulse to combine. Pour over crust and let cool at room temperature until set. Refrigerate until serving. Remove from pan, glaze and serve.

To prepare the glaze, blend strawberries and juice together until you have a nice purée and spoon over the top of the cake.

Blueberry Tart with Berry Glaze

Makes an 8 ½ inch tart

This tart is a striking bright purple colour and is topped with a fresh berry glaze and fresh blueberries. It is not overly sweet so add more sweetener if you like. Serve with a scoop of vanilla ice cream or Honey Peach Yogurt (pg. 282).

Crust

2 cups	oats, ground
¼ cup	fine shredded coconut, toasted
1 tsp	vanilla extract
⅓ cup	corn oil
¼ cup	honey

Filling

1 pkg	silken tofu, blue Mori Nu tetrapack
3 cups	frozen wild blueberries
½ cup	organic sugar
zest of 1	lemon
1 tsp	orange zest
2½ tbsp	arrowroot powder
1 tbsp	water
½ cup or so	fresh wild blueberries for garnish

Pre-heat oven to 350° F and lightly oil an 8½ spring form pan. To prepare the crust, combine ingredients together and press into the bottom of the pan. Bake for 15-20 minutes until golden brown. Remove from oven and set aside.

To prepare the filling, heat the blueberries, sugar and zests together until sugar is dissolved and the berries have begun to release their juice.

Remove from heat, strain and reserve excess juice. Purée the tofu in food processor or blender until creamy. Add the blueberries and 2 tablespoons of the arrowroot, blending until smooth. Taste and adjust sweetness if desired. Pour on top of the crust and bake for about 45 minutes until cake pulls away from the sides and the centre is set. Remove and allow to cool.

Combine the remaining arrowroot and water. In a small saucepan, bring to a simmer the reserved blueberry juice. Stir in the arrowroot mixture until thickened. Pour over top of cake, allow to cool and decorate with fresh berries and fresh edible flowers.

Lower your thermostat. For every 1 degree C you lower you save 2 % on your heating bill

Strawberry Shortcakes

Makes 1 dozen

Individual soft light cakes layered with Strawberry Cream (pg. 283) and sliced strawberries. Call it a very berry bonanza. Dehydrated strawberries can be found at the Bulk Barn and they are just bursting with concentrated flavour.

1½ cups	whole wheat flour
1½ cups +	all-purpose flour
1 tsp	baking powder
½ tsp	baking soda
½ cup	organic sugar
½ cup	unsalted butter, grated
2 cups	dehydrated strawberries
1 cup	buttermilk, plus 2 tbsp
2 tsp	vanilla extract
1 tsp	orange zest
2 cups	fresh strawberries, sliced

Pre-heat oven to 400° F and line a baking sheet with parchment paper. In a large bowl sift together the flours, baking powder and baking soda. Add the sugar and grated butter stirring to combine. Toss in dehydrated strawberries.

In a separate bowl combine the buttermilk, vanilla and orange zest. Add to the dry ingredients and stir to form a wet dough. Turn onto a lightly floured surface and knead for a minute or two, adding flour if necessary. Flatten and roll into a round about 1 inch thick. Using a 2 to 3 inch round cookie cutter, cut the dough into rounds and place cakes on baking sheet. Prick the tops once or twice with a fork and brush with remaining buttermilk. Bake for about 10 minutes or until puffy and golden brown.

To serve, slice shortcakes in half and layer strawberries, Strawberry Cream (pg. 283) and more strawberries. Top with remaining half and spoon cream over top so it trickles down the sides and finish with a strawberry on top.

Date Orange Almond Squares

Makes an 8 x 8 inch pan   VEGAN

Date squares are always popular. I have added a touch of citrus which enhances the flavour of the dates.

2 cups	dates, chopped
¾ cup	fresh squeezed orange juice
zest of 1	orange
2 cups	whole wheat flour
1 tsp	baking powder
¾ tsp	sea salt
½ cup	almonds, toasted & coarsely ground
½ cup	brown sugar
½ cup	unsalted butter, melted
1 tsp	lemon zest
¼ cup	almond milk

For a vegan alternative substitute vegetable oil for the butter.

Pre-heat oven to 350º F and lightly butter/oil an 8 x 8 inch baking dish. In a small pot over medium heat combine the dates, orange juice and orange zest stirring until dates are smooth. Set aside. In a large bowl combine dry ingredients. In a separate bowl whisk together butter, lemon zest and almond milk. Add to the dry mix stirring until you have a nice crumbly dough.

Press ⅔ of the dough into bottom of the pan. Smooth the date mixture on top of the dough and crumble the remaining dough over the dates. Bake for 25 to 35 minutes or until golden brown. Allow to cool and then cut into squares.

LEMON COCONUT SQUARES

Makes an 8 x 8 inch pan.

A "lemony" coconut treat just like grandma used to make. Well that's what a guest remarked about these yummy squares.

Base
1½ cups	all-purpose flour
½ cup	unsweetened shredded coconut, toasted
½ tsp	baking powder
¼ cup	organic sugar
½ cup	oats
½ cup	unsalted butter, melted
1 tsp	lemon zest
1 tsp	vanilla extract

Filling
1 cup	unsweetened shredded coconut, toasted
2	eggs, separated
¾ cup	organic sugar
zest of 3½	lemons
½ cup	lemon juice
¼ tsp	sea salt
2 tbsp	all-purpose flour

Pre-heat oven to 350° F and lightly butter an 8 x 8 baking dish.

To make the base, combine all ingredients in a bowl and then press into pan. Bake for 15 minutes until fragrant and golden. Remove and set aside.

To make the filling, combine coconut, egg yolks, ½ cup sugar, lemon juice, zest and sea salt. In a separate bowl whip the egg whites and remaining ¼ cup sugar with a mixer until foamy and peaks form. Fold into the egg yolk mixture until just combined. Pour over base and bake for about 35 minutes or until set and firm.

Energy Burst Granola Bars

Makes an 8 x 8 inch pan

Packed with nutrients and energy, these bars are sure to take you through your day.

¾ cup	dates, chopped fine
¼ cup	prunes, chopped fine
¼ cup	water
½ cup	unsalted butter or safflower oil
½ cup	honey
⅓ cup	almond butter
2 tsp	vanilla extract
1½ tsp	cinnamon
3 cups	rolled oats
pinch	sea salt
¼ cup each	raisins, chopped figs & sunflower seeds
½ cup	sliced almonds

Pre-heat oven to 350° F and lightly oil the baking pan. In a small saucepan over medium low heat, combine the dates, prunes and water and stir until a smooth paste is formed. Add the butter or oil, honey and almond butter stirring until well combined. Stir in the vanilla.

In a large bowl, combine dry ingredients, then add liquid mixture and stir well. Spoon mixture into prepared pan and bake about 20 minutes or until golden brown. Allow to cool before slicing.

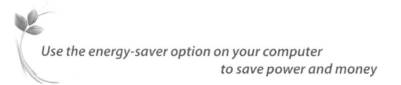

Use the energy-saver option on your computer to save power and money

Strawberry Bars

ᴠᴇɢᴀɴ

These bars are a pretty treat come strawberry season but you could substitute any berry or fruit depending on the season.

Base

2 cups	rolled oats
¾ cup	spelt flour
6 tbsp	agave nectar
½ cup	canola oil
2 tsp	vanilla extract
½ tsp	nutmeg

Topping

¾ cup	strawberry jam
2 cups	fresh strawberries, stems removed & sliced
1 cup	apple juice
½ cup	strawberry or cherry juice
2 tbsp	agar flakes
2 tbsp	arrowroot powder mixed with 2 tbsp water

Pre-heat oven to 350° F. Press a piece of parchment paper into an 8 x 8 inch pan overlapping the sides, this is to lift the bars out of the pan. Combine base ingredients together and lightly press into pan. Bake for 15 minutes and let cool. Spread jam over base and layer the sliced strawberries on top.

In a small saucepan, combine the agar and juice and bring to a boil. Reduce heat and simmer for 5-8 minutes until the agar has dissolved. Add the arrowroot and stir until thickened. Remove from heat and pour over the strawberries. Cool at room temperature and then refrigerate until set. Remove and slice into bars.

ALMOND BUTTER FLAX COOKIES

Makes 17 large   VEGAN

These cookies are soft and chewy and also egg and dairy free.
Substitute spelt flour for the whole wheat if you prefer. Choose vegan
chocolate chips or carob chips for a vegan alternative.

1	large ripe banana, mashed
4 tsp	ground flax mixed with ¼ cup water
2 tsp	vanilla extract
2 tbsp	corn oil
⅝ cup	almond butter
⅓ cup	sucanat
1 cup	whole wheat flour
2 tsp	baking powder
½ tsp	baking soda
¼ tsp	sea salt
¼ tsp	nutmeg
½ cup	sliced almonds
½ cup	chocolate chips, optional

Pre-heat oven to 350° F and line a baking sheet with parchment paper.
In a food processor, combine the wet ingredients and the sucanat;
blend until creamy. In a separate bowl sift together the flour, baking
powder and baking soda and then add remaining ingredients. Add
wet mix to dry and stir until combined. Drop large spoonfuls of dough
onto the baking sheet and bake for about 17 minutes until golden on
the bottom.

Don't let the faucet run while you clean vegetables.

QUINOA GINGER COOKIES

Makes 15

These cookies were inspired by leftover quinoa and an abundance of ginger. They are cake-like with a lovely ginger flavour and not overly sweet. See glossary on how to cook quinoa.

¼ cup	unsalted butter
¼ cup	olive oil
½ cup	sucanat
1	egg
2 tsp	vanilla extract
½ cup	cooked quinoa
1 large tbsp	freshly ground ginger
1 cup	all-purpose flour
1 tsp	baking powder
¼ tsp	baking soda
¼ tsp	pink Himalayan salt
¼ tsp	dried ground ginger
handful	pine nuts for garnish

Pre-heat oven to 350° F and line a baking sheet with parchment paper. In a food processor, blend the butter and oil together until creamy. Add sucanat and blend for a couple of minutes until sucanat begins to break down. Add the egg, vanilla, quinoa and ginger and pulse until creamy, about 10 seconds.

In a separate bowl stir together dry ingredients. Add wet ingredients to dry and stir to combine fully. Spoon onto baking sheet about 1 inch apart and lightly press 3 or 4 pinenuts into each cookie. Bake for about 15 minutes or until bottom of cookie is golden.

CRANBERRY ORANGE SUNFLOWER COOKIES

Makes 22 large cookies

These cookies will satisfy your sweet tooth and keep you going throughout the day. Make sure the butter and eggs are room temperature.

¾ cup	unsalted butter
¼ cup	sunflower or safflower oil
¼ cup	rice syrup
½ cup	honey
2	eggs
1 tsp	vanilla extract
1 tsp	orange extract
2 cups	whole wheat flour
1½ cups	oats
1 tsp	sea salt
2 tsp	baking powder
⅛ tsp	ground cloves
zest of 1	orange
1 cup	sunflower seeds
1 cup	dried cranberries

Vegan option- substitute flax eggs, see glossary. Omit butter and use all oil. Use agave nectar for the honey.

Pre-heat oven to 350° F and line baking sheet with parchment paper. Cream together butter, oil, rice syrup and honey in a food processor until smooth. Add eggs one at a time, blending well after each one. Add the extracts.

In a large bowl combine dry ingredients and add to wet stirring until mixed together. Scoop about a ¼ cup of dough per cookie and place on the baking sheet flattening slightly with a fork. Bake for 20 minutes until golden brown.

CHOCOLATE MINT COOKIES

Makes about 20 large cookies

Chocolate and mint are a classic combination. Enjoy.

½ cup	unsalted butter
¼ cup	sunflower or safflower oil
½ cup	honey
2	eggs
1 tsp	vanilla extract
1½ tsp	mint extract
2 cups	whole wheat flour
¾ cup	oats
2 tsp	baking powder
½ tsp	sea salt
½ cup	cocoa powder, sifted
1 cup	semi sweet chocolate chips

Pre-heat oven to 350° F and line a baking sheet with parchment paper. In a food processor cream together butter, oil and honey until smooth. Add eggs one at a time blending well after each one. Add vanilla and mint and pulse to combine.

In a large bowl combine dry ingredients. Add wet ingredients to dry and stir until combined. Using an ice cream scoop or a large spoon scoop about a ¼ cup of dough per cookie and place on the baking sheet flattening slightly with a fork. Bake for about 15 minutes. Cookies will be soft be firm up as they sit.

GRANOLA NUGGETS

Makes about 20

A high energy blast in a mouthful. Versatile and easy to make.

½ cup	dates, chopped
½ cup	Thompsons raisins
½ cup	walnuts, toasted
¼ cup	dried prunes
¼ cup	dried apricots
¼ cup	dried cranberries
3 tbsp	fresh squeezed orange juice
2 tsp	orange zest
½ cup	oats, ground fine
½ cup	unsweetened fine coconut, toasted

Place dates, raisins, walnuts, prunes, apricots and cranberries in the food processor and mince until fine. Add the juice and zest and blend again.

Place the oats on one plate and the coconut on another. Dampen hands slightly and form mixture into teaspoon size balls. Roll in either the coconut or the oats.

Eliminate "phantom drains" by unplugging electrical equipment and appliances when not in use

TROPICAL FRUIT PUDDING

Serves 2-4

This is a refreshing dessert that children love and is super easy to make. It has the consistency of a jello-like pudding with its sweetness coming primarily from the fruit juice and a small touch of honey. Try also serving for breakfast with granola sprinkled on top.

1½ cups	natural Tropical Fruit juice
1½ tbsp	agar flakes
2 tbsp	arrowroot powder mixed with 2 tbsp water
½ cup	plain 3% yogurt, gelatin free
2 tbsp	honey or to taste
½ cup	wild blueberries
½ cup	pineapple, diced

Have ready individual ramekin dishes lined with the blueberries and pineapple. Alternatively make one large dessert using a 4 x 8 inch loaf pan.

In a small saucepan heat the juice and agar to boiling stirring continuously. Reduce heat to low and simmer about 5-8 minutes until agar is dissolved. Add the arrowroot mixture and stir until thickened about 10 seconds. Add the yogurt and honey and stir to combine. Pour over the fruit and allow to cool at room temperature and then refrigerate until set.

Yogurt Finales

These are alternatives to ice cream and whipped cream. Substitute soy yogurt for a vegan alternative, adjusting sweetness to taste. Use any type of plain natural yogurt as long as it is gelatin free.

Maple Yogurt "Cream"

1 cup	plain yogurt
1 tsp	pure vanilla extract
2 tbsp	pure maple syrup – or to taste

Combine all ingredients in a small bowl and refrigerate.

Honey Peach Yogurt Sauce

1 cup	plain yogurt
1 tbsp	honey or to taste
1 cup	fresh peaches, peeled & pitted
¼ tsp	lime zest

Blend all ingredients together until smooth and refrigerate.

Strawberry Yogurt Sauce

1 cup	plain yogurt
1 tbsp	agave nectar
1 cup	frozen strawberries

Prepare as per Honey Peach Yogurt.

Tofu Creams

You can use these creams on their own as a pudding, to make eclairs by filling Choux Puff Pastry (pg. 85) or as icing on a cake. Adding the xanthan gum thickens the creams and holds them together better. I prefer Mori Nu tetra pack brand, but any silken brand will work fine.

Strawberry Almond Cream

½ pkg	silken tofu, about 6 oz
1 cup	frozen strawberries
½ cup	organic sugar
½ tsp	almond extract
½ tsp	xanthan gum

Place tofu in food processor and purée until smooth with no lumps. Add remaining ingredients and blend until sugar is dissolved. Chill until serving.

Chocolate "Icing"

1 pkg	silken tofu
1 cup	melted semi sweet chocolate or chipits
1 tsp	vanilla extract

Blend together until smooth.

Date "Icing"

See Date Fruit Cake (pg. 253)

APPENDIX

WELCOME TO A HARMONY DAWN WEEKEND MENU PLAN

Friday Dinner- Southeast Asian
Indonesian Tempeh and vegetable curry over sweet black rice
Warm salad of seasonal vegetables and organic greens with Indonesian Salad Dressing
Baked vegetable spring rolls with sweet chili dipping sauce
Tea Selection
Coconut Chocolate Banana "Cheesecake"

Saturday Breakfast
Macadamia, Pecan & Cranberry Granola with side of yogurt, soy and regular milk
Pecan, Banana Buttermilk Pancakes with warm buttered pears & local maple syrup
Platter of seasonal fresh fruit- oranges, apples, grapes, bananas, grapefruit, peaches etc.
Strawberry Walnut Muffins with strawberry butter
Basket of homemade breads with choice of preserves
Tea Selection and Organic fair trade coffee

Saturday Lunch- Mediterranean Cuisine
Leek and Potato Soup
Grilled Antipasti Salad with Arugula Pesto
Organic Greens tossed with Italian Vinaigrette & toasted sunflower seeds
Pine nut Rosemary and onion Foccacia Buns
Quinoa and Ginger Cookies
Tea selection

Saturday Dinner – Chinese Cuisine
Easy Egg Drop Soup
Kong Hei Fat Choy Stir fry over Sweet Pea Fried Rice
Seared Garlic Ginger Sesame Tofu Steaks
Sichuan Green Beans
Tea Selection
Tropical Fruit Pudding

Sunday Breakfast

Warm 12 grain cereal with apples, raisins, goji berries
Fresh fruit salad with mango, watermelon, oranges and lime zest
Scrambled local farm eggs with scallions and fresh garden herbs
Tomato Parmesan Scones with herb butter
Basket of homemade breads with choice of preserves
Tea Selection and Organic fair trade coffee

Sunday Lunch- Mexican Cuisine

Quesadilla Platter- Black Bean and Avocado Quesadillas and Spicy Corn
Quesadillas served with condiments of sour cream and tomato salsa
Jade rice pilaf
Romaine leaves tossed with Lemon Parmesan Parsley Dressing
Sliced Garden Tomatoes sprinkled with olive oil, coarse salt and herbs
Ontario Summer Fruit Flan
Tea Selection

GLOSSARY

Adzuki beans - or aduki are small, reddish beans from China. They are easier to digest than other beans and have a mild to sweet flavour. They are used in Asian desserts as well as savoury dishes.

Agar Agar - a thickening agent made from a sea vegetable. It comes in powder form, flakes and bars. It dissolves in hot water or broth, or you can sprinkle into sauces and dressings while blending to thicken. It gels together upon cooling. It has no flavour and is a natural alternative to gelatin. If using flakes, 1 tbsp per cup of liquid.

Agave Nectar - liquid sweetener made from the agave cactus plant native to Mexico. It is neutral in flavour, dissolves quickly and pours faster than honey. It can be found at health stores and some large grocery stores.

Arame - a species of kelp characterized by long strands. It is somewhat sweet in comparison to other sea vegetables. High in calcium and iron but also contains alginate and iodine. Cover with cold water for 10 minutes to reconstitute and then drain. Use in salads, stir fries, soups.

Arrowroot - used as a thickener and substitute for cornstarch measure for measure. It is a starch from a root similar to the cassava plant. It dissolves in cool liquid to form a paste but must be brought to a boil to thicken. Continued boiling dissipates its thickening ability.

Baking Powder - a leavening powder that is a mixture of alkaline and acid. It will leaven a batter without the addition of an acid. Double acting baking powder reacts with liquid to initiate the leavening process and then again in the oven when the batter is exposed to heat. Most commonly used when recipes contain no acidic ingredients.

Baking Soda - an alkaline powder used for leavening. Baking soda must react with an acid such as buttermilk, citrus juice, yogurt, sour milk, molasses, honey or cocoa powder in order to leaven the baked goods. Just a small amount is needed to react with the acids of other ingredients. For example only a ½ tsp of baking soda for every 1 cup of buttermilk or yogurt.

Barley Malt Syrup - a dark sweetener with a consistency thicker than molasses. It can be used to replace honey and molasses in most baked goods. It is half as sweet as white sugar and needs to be refrigerated.

Beans - in a large pot, cover dried beans with lots of water and soak for at least 8 hours. Drain, rinse and add enough water to cover beans by about 3 inches. Add a piece of kombu, bring to a boil and simmer until beans are tender. Cooking times vary. See Legumes (pg. 58) for more information.

Black Beans Sauce - a bottled Chinese condiment of fermented black beans, rice wine and garlic. They have a salty taste.

Blanch - a method of cooking where you plunge food into boiling water briefly and then into cold water. Also helps to loosen the skins of tomatoes, nectarines, plums and peaches.

Bonito Flakes - known as katsuo-bushi in Japanese cuisine. They are flakes of dried smoked bonito fish which is a kind of tuna. A seasoning used to make katsuo-bushi dashi which is a Japanese broth.

Bragg Liquid Aminos - a substitute for soy sauce and tamari. It has a savoury and salty flavour. It contains liquid amino acids and is can be found at health stores and major food stores.

Brown Rice Syrup - a thick, liquid sweetener with a mild taste and is a sugar substitute. Refrigerate to prevent surface mold.

Bulgur (Bulghur) Wheat - Middle Eastern staple is precooked wheat that has been steamed and dried, then cracked into small pieces. It is fast cooking.

Capers - small buds that are usually pickled, they are used in salads, with smoked salmon and as a garnish.

Carob - the dark brown pod of the Mediterranean evergreen known as locust tree. It is used as a coffee substitute and is caffeine free. Available in powder and chips. Sold in health stores.

Chiffonade - a way of cutting fine strips out of green leafy vegetables. Roll the leaves into a cigar shape and then slice crosswise into thin strips.

Chili Oil - very spicy blend of dried chili peppers, cayenne, garlic and vegetable oil. Available at Asian markets. I use Manna brand and a drop is all you need.

Chili Paste - a concentrated thick paste of ground chilis, garlic and oil. Sold in small jars in most supermarkets.

Chinese Five-Spice Powder - a pungent spice blend of cinnamon, cloves, fennel seed, star anise and Szechuan peppercorns. A little is all you need.

Chipotle Peppers - a smoked jalapeno chili pepper with a smoky sweet flavour. Available dried and pickled but I mostly use in canned form in adobo sauce.

Coconut Milk - available canned, powdered and creamed. I use the canned form as it has a thick creamy consistency.

Coconut Oil* - is a nutritionally beneficial fat. It is antimicrobial, antibacterial, antifungal, anti-inflammatory and loaded with antioxidants. It contains lauric acid, also found in mother's milk and contributes to a healthy immune system. You can use it in place of canola or vegetable oil for sautéing, especially with stir-fries and curries. Recommended brands include Spectrum, Omega, Tropical Traditions.*source, Fran McCullough author of The Good Fat Cookbook.

Couscous - generally made from precooked refined wheat. Cooks in about 3 minutes.

Curry Paste - a blend of ingredients made with garlic, chilies, ginger, hot peppers, lemongrass, oil and seasonings. Used to enhance and bring out the flavours of the dish. Thai curries come in yellow, red and green with green being the hottest. Indian curries come in mild, medium and hot. Sold in jars at your local supermarket.

Date Puree - a sweetener that I use a lot with chocolate desserts. In a saucepan heat 1 cup of chopped pitted dates with ¼ cup water until smooth. Proceed with recipe.

Daikon - a large long white or green radish with a spicy taste.

Dulse - sea vegetable from the Atlantic with a red/purple leaves. It is mild with a salty taste and can be found in leaf and flake form. Used for sprinkling over vegetables, salads, rice and is nutrient rich.

Emulsify - a technique which forces two liquids which aren't compatible together to form one. Emulsifiers are substances that are soluble in both water and fat which link the two together to form a bond.

Fish Sauce - a Southeast Asian sauce made from salted and fermented anchovies. Has a pungent smell but brings out the flavour of the dish.

Flax Eggs - a substitute in baking for eggs. Flax meal or ground flax mixed with water gels together and forms a binding action similar to eggs. 1 tsp of flax meal with 2 tbsp warm water = 1 egg.

Furikake Seasonings - a blend of minced nori seaweed, sesame seeds and spices. It can be found in Asian markets.

Garam Masala - a blend of aromatic Indian spices, usually dry roasted and then ground fine. Black pepper, cinnamon, cardamom, cloves, cumin, chilies, fennel, nutmeg, mace may be included in the blend.

Gelatin - a thickening agent made from collagen, a protein found in animal connective tissue and bones. Used in many commercially processed foods to make them appear thicker and creamier such as yogurt, dressings, sauces, jello etc. Agar agar works just as well without the yuck factor.

Gremolata - is a mixture of seasonings used in sauces or on soups. Concentrated in flavour so a little goes a long way.

Herbs - usage - rule of thumb is ½ tsp dried for every 1 tbsp of fresh

Herbes de Provence - is a blend of rosemary, marjoram, thyme, savory, basil, lavender and sage. It is used mostly in stews, sauces and bourguignon.

Hijiki - thick strands of calcium rich dried black seaweed stronger in flavour than Arame. Soak in warm water for about 30 minutes to reconstitute. It holds its shape in dishes.

Hoisin Sauce - a sweet, thick sauce used in Chinese cooking. Made from soybeans, garlic, chilies, sugar, vinegar or other citrus juices

Kaffir Lime Leaves - dark green, highly aromatic leaves with a strong citrus smell and flavour. Commonly used in Indonesian cooking and can be found fresh, frozen or dried. If unavailable, you can substitute 1 ½ tsp of grated lime zest for each lime leaf.

Kecap Manis - is a sweet soy sauce with garlic, Szechuan peppercorns, anise and citrus, available at Asian markets.

Kombu - flat broad thick seaweed used to flavour broths.

Lemongrass - hard, thick pale green stalks of grass used primarily in

Southeast Asian cooking. Remove the outer leaves and bruise with a rolling pin to bring out the flavour. Use only the bottom few inches. Can be minced into a paste or used whole in stews and soups. Remove prior to serving. Found in Asian markets and some supermarkets. Freezes well.

Liquid Smoke - smoky liquid found in bottled form used to add a smoky flavour to sauces or dressings. Use conservatively, a little goes a long way.

Marmite - a yeast extract that is very nutritious and loaded with B vitamins. Used as a seasoning for soups, stews, broths and on toast. British in origin.

Millet - a mild grain with a nutty flavour. Small and round with a yellow colour. It is easier to digest than other grains and is nearly a complete protein.

Mirin - a sweet Japanese cooking wine made from rice that adds flavour to dishes.

Miso - a naturally aged fermented soybean paste used in soups, stews, sauces and dressings. It is salty, high in protein and enzymes and full of flavour. Miso comes in a range of flavours and colours and can be mixed with rice, grains or wine to create different flavours. Its live enzymes are destroyed if boiled.

Nori - dark green seaweed that is sold in sheets and most commonly used for making sushi but can be shredded and served over salads or crushed and tossed into stews and soup. High in vitamins and minerals.

Nutritional Yeast - is considered a dietary supplement and has a cheesy taste. It is a good source of protein and B vitamins. Used as a seasoning that can be added to soups, stews, burgers, popcorn etc.

Parchment Paper - heat resistant and stick free paper used in cooking and baking to line the pans.

Pre-heat - to turn the oven on about 15 minutes a head of time to heat the oven and allow it to reach its set temperature.

Proof - to proof means to test baking yeast to make sure it is alive. Adding yeast to warm water with a touch of honey makes the yeast foam and bubble signifying life.

Puff Pastry - soft, sweet and puffy when baked. Time consuming to make on your own. It is available in blocks, frozen from the supermarket.

Quinoa - an ancient grain grown by the Incas in Peru and pronounced "Keenwa". It is a complete source of protein and high in calcium and other minerals. It has a mild yet nutty flavour and light texture. Versatile and easy to digest it resembles Saturn with a little ring around it. Available in beige and red varieties. Needs to be rinsed well to remove saponin which is a natural preservative but has a slightly bitter taste. Easy to cook, bring water to a boil, add a touch of salt along with the quinoa and simmer covered for 15 minutes until water is absorbed. Remove from heat and spread out onto a baking sheet to steam. This prevents clumping. Water ratio is ½ cup quinoa to 1 cup water, 1 cup quinoa to 2 cups water and so forth

Roasting Garlic - slice the top off the garlic bulb to reveal garlic and sprinkle with salt and pepper and olive oil. Place in a foil pouch and roast in a 400° F oven for about 30 to 45 minutes until soft and fragrant. When cooled gently squeeze out of bulb.

Roasting Peppers - place peppers in oven or on a barbeque and roast at 400° F turning as each side blackens. Remove when black and place in a bowl covered with a plate to allow the peppers to sweat and cool, for about 15 minutes. Skin will rub off, core and remove seeds.

Sambal Oelek - a super hot Asian chile pepper paste or sauce.

Seitan - or Buddhists Meat is made from marinated wheat gluten and can be used in stir fries, stews, sandwiches etc. It is chewy and has a high protein content. You can make your own (see section on Seitan in Building Blocks) or purchase ready-made from a health food store.

Sesame Oil - most commonly purchased as toasted sesame oil. It has a distinctive aroma and is used for flavouring rather than as a cooking oil. A little goes a long way as it can overpower a dish but used sparingly it lends a wonderful flavour to dishes, dressings and sauces.

Shiitake Mushrooms - available fresh or dried. They are cultivated large Japanese mushrooms with a chewy texture and meaty earthy flavour. To reconstitute, place dried mushrooms in a pot of water and bring to a boil. Simmer for about 15 minutes, turn off heat and let sit another 15 minutes. Discard stems and proceed. Retain broth for other uses in soups, sauces or dressings.

Silken Tofu - a smooth silky variety of tofu that is often found in tetra packs from Mori-Nu (the brand I prefer). It is ideal for sauces, dressings and desserts.

Soba Noodles - Japanese noodles made from buckwheat and wheat flours. Ideal for soups.

Star Anise - native to China, it is shaped like an eight pointed star with a licorice flavour.

Sucanat - a natural sweetener defined as Sugar Cane Natural. A substitute for brown sugar but with more of a molasses flavour.

Tamarind Paste - brown pods that are sour in taste. Can be purchased dried or as a puree or concentrate.

Tahini - a thick, smooth paste made from ground sesame seeds. Used in dips, dressings, sauces and desserts. A good thickener in sauces.

Tamari - a naturally brewed soy sauce made from fermented soybeans that doesn't contain any additives or sugar. It is available wheat free and is salty in flavour.

Tapioca Starch Flour - gluten free it is the flour made from the root of the cassava plant. It is mostly used as a thickener and is similar to arrowroot and cornstarch.

Tempeh - native to Indonesia, it is a soy food that is fermented and sold in blocks. Not to be eaten raw. Marinated and cooked, it is extremely versatile.

Turmeric - a spice with a bright yellow orange colour and pungent flavour. Sold dried, it comes from the root of a tropical plant similar to ginger. Used in South Asian cooking (curries), it can also be added as a colouring agent to desserts. Considered an anti-inflammatory spice and excellent for the maintenance of good health.

Umeboshi - vinegar & paste- made from Japanese sour plums and are thought to aid digestion. High in vitamins and minerals.

Wood Ears - dried black fungi also known as Cloud Ears or Tree Ears. They expand to look like black flowers with a crunchy exterior texture and a mild subtle flavour. They can be found in Asian markets. Soak in hot water for 30 minutes to reconstitute.

Worcestershire Sauce - a condiment made with anchovies, garlic, soy, tamarind, onions, molasses, vinegar and seasonings. A vegetarian version is available at health stores.

Xanthan Gum - and Guar Gum are natural binders, like an egg for instance. When mixed with a low gluten flour, they bind with the gluten in the flour and help it to rise. They are readily available at health food stores and at the Bulk Barn.

RESOURCES

Anti cancer: A New Way of Life, David Servan-Schreiber, M.D., Ph.D, Harper Collins, 2007.

Prescription for Nutritional Healing-Fourth Edition, Phyllis A. Balch, Penguin Group, 2006

The Science of Good Food, David Joachim and Andrew Schloss, Robert Rose Publishing, 2008

The Food Connection, Sam Graci, Macmillian Publishing 2001

A Call to Women: The Healthy Breast Program & Workbook, Sat Dharam Kaur, ND, Quarry Health Books 2001

The End of Food: How the Food Industry is Destroying our Food Supply & What We Can Do About It, Thomas F. Pawlick, Greystone Books, 2006

Renewable Energy Handbook: A guide to Rural Energy Independence, Off-grid & Sustainable Living, William H. Kemp, Aztext Press, 2005

The Weather Makers: How we are changing the climate & what it means for life on earth, Tim Flannery, Harper Collins, 2005

A Theory of Everything: An Intergral Vision for Business, Politics, Science and Spirituality, Ken Wilber, Shambhala Publications Inc., 2000

Ecoholic (when you're addicted to the planet), Adria Vasil, Random House, 2007

BOOKS BY THE AUTHORS

Ageless Wisdom Spirituality: Investing in Human Evolution, Andy James, Xlibris, 2003
The Conscious I: Clarity and Direction Through Meditation, Andy James, Summerville House, 1992
Spiritual Legacy of the Shaolin Temple: Buddhism, Daoism and the Energetic Arts, Andy James, Wisdom Publications, 2004
Dao of Harmony Dawn Cooking: Innovative and Acclaimed Spa Cuisine, Nicola Lawrence, First Choice Publishing, 2007

INDEX

CONVERSION CHART

Measurements and Conversions

I have used the Imperial standard form of measurement which is cups, tablespoons, teaspoons, pounds and Fahrenheit. I have not listed metric measurements due to spacing on the page and to save any confusion. Below is an approximate equivalent of converting back and forth to metric.

Common abbreviations used throughout the book are:

tsp	=	*teaspoon*
tbsp	=	*tablespoon*
oz.	=	*ounce*
1b	=	*pound*

Imperial Dry

3 tsp	=	*1 tbsp*
4 tbsp	=	*¼ cup*
16 tbsp	=	*1 cup*

Imperial Volume (Liquid)

4 oz	=	*½ cup*		
8 oz	=	*1 cup*	=	*½ pint*
16 oz	=	*2 cups*	=	*1 pint*
32 oz	=	*4 cups*	=	*1 quart*

Metric Conversion

1 tsp	=	*5 ml*
3 tsp	=	*15 ml*
¼ cup	=	*62 ml (approx)*
½ cup	=	*125 ml (approx)*
1 cup	=	*250 ml (approx) = ¼ litre*
4 cups	=	*1000 ml = 1 litre*
1 oz	=	*30 grams (approx)*
½ lb	=	*225 grams (approx)*
1 lb	=	*450 grams (approx)*
2.2 lb	=	*1 kg*

Equivalents and Substitutions

1 stick of butter = 8 tbsp = ½ cup
½ tbsp cornstarch = 1 tbsp flour used for thickening
1 tbsp flour = 1 ½ tbsp arrowroot and tapioca flour, used for thickening
1 tbsp gelatin = 1 tbsp agar in powder form
1 tsp sea salt = 2 tbsp miso or 3 tbsp tamari
¾ cup white sugar = ½ cup maple syrup or ½ cup honey or ¾ cup brown sugar or 1 ½ cups brown rice syrup
1 tsp dried herbs = 1 tbsp freshly chopped herbs
1 clove garlic = ¼ tsp garlic powder

About the Authors and Harmony Dawn

Harmony Dawn is a beautiful, secluded, rural Ontario retreat, celebrated for its unique, energetic and environmental vision and design, and especially for its innovative, vegetarian spa cuisine. Yin-Yang principles are used to create a healing sense of tranquility and flow within and around the retreat building, which incorporates a variety of sustainable technologies including wind and solar power. Guests have the rare opportunity to experience for themselves what a cleaner, greener, and more aware future might feel like … and taste like. Overwhelmingly, they love it!

Harmony Dawn caters to groups of 8-22 people and has proven extremely popular with guests concerned with whole health, the environment, arts and personal transformation disciplines like meditation, Tai Chi, Qigong, yoga and more.

Nicola Lawrence is Harmony Dawn's chef and co-founder. Her delicious, artistically colourful, tantalizing and always satisfying cuisine is the distillation of many years' experience in Toronto's food industry, vegetarian cooking, Yin-Yang theory and subtle energy (Qi or prana). She is a Feng Shui consultant, Medical Qigong Practitioner (MQP) and an ardent student of Tai Chi Chuan. Her first book, *The Dao of Harmony Dawn Cooking: Innovative and Acclaimed Spa Cuisine,* is a smash hit (one reader cooked every single recipe in the book) and Harmony Dawn's guests are always more than willing (and elated) to taste-test her new creations.

Andy James is a renowned mind-body teacher, author of 4 books, Qigong healer, and martial arts master, who has represented Canada. A former Chartered Accountant who made a dramatic career change, Andy has been teaching in the greater Toronto area for 25 years and is the founder of the well-known Tai Chi and Meditation Centre and with Nicola Lawrence, of Harmony Dawn retreat. For more information on Andy and his considerable and innovative body of work on mind-body and environmental integration, alternative health and the "internal arts", check out www.torontotaichimeditationcentre.com and www.andyjames.ca. Andy is also a member of the Forge Institute (www.theforge.org), which promotes trans-traditional spirituality, and he is a co-director and one of the authors of the

Forge's global initiative, www.globalspiritualcitizenship.org

Andy James, Nicola Lawrence and Harmony Dawn have been featured many times on local, national and international media, including TV, radio, magazines and newspapers.

For more information on Harmony Dawn, Nicola and Andy, or to book a retreat, buy or be added to our mailing list, go to www.harmonydawn.com